Typologies of Delinquency
A Critical Analysis

STUDIES IN SOCIOLOGY

Consulting Editor:

ROBERT NISBET,
University of California,
Riverside

Typologies of Delinquency

A Critical Analysis

THEODORE N. FERDINAND

Northeastern University

RANDOM HOUSE · NEW YORK

Dedication

Most authors owe a word of thanks to a multitude of teachers and colleagues without whom their own work would have been impossible. The two scholars to whom I owe the most gratitude are Morris Janowitz and Guy E. Swanson. Neither had anything to do with this work, but both had a great deal to do with my understanding of human behavior. Without them, these ideas might never have occurred to me.

Acknowledgments

A number of my friends and colleagues have graciously helped me at various points in the drafting of this work. Irwin Goldberg read nearly all the manuscript and gave many careful and valuable suggestions. Harold Zamansky and Lee Macht read Chapter Five and helped resolve several difficult problems. James Teele and Morton Rubin offered many useful suggestions regarding Chapter Four, and Edward Hacker helped me clarify some of the problems discussed in Chapter Three. The late Herbert Bloch as an editor of Random House read the first three chapters, and his successor, Robert Nisbet, read the entire manuscript. Both men made many insightful suggestions regarding style and content, and my students at Northeastern suffered through the formulation of these ideas with admirable patience and intelligent criticism. Finally, my wife, Jane, read the entire work with a careful eye and helped, thereby, to avoid many errors and malapropisms. All of these contributed very generously to whatever merit this study may possess and deserve my sincere thanks.

Contents

Typologies of Delinquency
A Critical Analysis

CHAPTER 1

A Jurisdictional Dispute

Perhaps no other issue since the birth of the behavioral sciences has provoked more contentious debate than that concerning the causes of delinquency and crime. Currently, the battle lines are drawn broadly between (1) those who insist that delinquency in both substance and cause is basically social and, therefore, not amenable to psychological or physiological explanation and (2) those who maintain that delinquency is in the last analysis an empirical problem and that any factor—whether social, psychological, or physiological—can be utilized in explaining delinquency, as long as it is demonstrably related to the problem.

The Purists, which is the name I shall give to those who maintain that the problem is essentially social in nature, derive much of their inspiration from Durkheim's famous assertion that "The determining cause of a social fact should be sought among the social facts that preceded it and not among the states of the individual consciousness."[1] They insist that delinquency and other allied problems are ultimately rooted in social processes and that to explain them in terms of psychological or physiological factors is merely to confuse what is most immediate to delinquent behavior with what is most significant. They agree that the behavior of delinquents and, indeed, of all humans is an expression of personal likes and dislikes; but these personal preferences, they maintain, are themselves guided and even inspired by socially defined structures. Thus, the individual's personality is simply a medium through which social processes unfold, and to explain human behavior it is only necessary to establish why the social environment is structured as it is and why some people get involved with certain facets of their social environment and not others. Delinquency for the Purists, therefore, is a kind of socially patterned behavior that depends very little upon the personal idiosyncrasies—psychological or physiological—of the individual.

The Empiricists, on the other hand, typically proceed without the benefit of any over-all theoretical framework, energetically uncovering new relationships wherever found. They appear to resent the restraint that a formal theory would impose, preferring instead to survey the delinquent universe before developing any abstract generalizations or theoretical explanations. In the last analysis the value of their work is governed primarily by the sophistication of their methodology and the quality of their intuitions.

The Purists chastise the Empiricists for their unprincipled eclecticism, whereas the Empiricists doggedly maintain that it is folly to speculate about the causes of delinquency before its precise nature has been carefully assayed. In recent years the Purists have been skillfully represented by Sutherland and his disciples, and the Empiricists have been most recently defended by the Gluecks.

Amid the din and confusion of debate, however, a basic problem can be dimly outlined. At issue, basically, is the significance of the relationships that are uncovered between delinquency and factors at nonsocial levels of analysis. No one seems to feel uncomfortable when attributing a causal role to social factors or processes, but a skirmish quickly develops when psychological or physiological factors are reported as being related to delinquency and not specifically designated as dependent variables. Generally, the Purists have responded to studies linking delinquency with psychological or constitutional factors, first, by pointing to the lack of consensus in the hundreds of studies that have asserted such relationships, and, second, by hinting rather strongly that delinquency may, indeed, be the independent variable after all.[2] Essentially, their objective is to establish the primacy of social processes, deriving all else from them.

The Empiricists for their part have generally not been cautious about mixing different levels of analysis in explaining delinquency. They have been quite willing to mingle several kinds of causal factors while paying little heed to the need for a logical framework to guide their speculations. William Healy, Cyril Burt, and Lowell J. Carr are all well-known for their willingness to approach delinquency with an "open" mind, but it is the Gluecks who have pursued this policy most diligently and given it its most recent formulation. Consider, for example, the following admonition:

> It must also be borne in mind that etiologic influence is typically multiple and complex, consisting of numerous traits and factors of which each is but a part of the causal nexus. It is very doubtful whether, standing alone, any single trait or factor analyzed in this study would be sufficient to account for delinquency. Moreover, while "cause" requires a totality of influences indispensable to the result, it cannot be exactly

determined how much weight each of the traits contributes to any theoretical total causal influence.[3]

It is clear from this excerpt, and from other portions of their work as well, that the Gluecks see several essentially different kinds of traits, factors, or processes combining in some fashion to produce delinquency. More recently, however, they have narrowed the causal complex down to just two types of factors, the constitutional and the social.[4] They speculate that these two types of factors participate in controlling the individual's characteristics in three main ways: some characteristics are shaped primarily by constitutional factors, others stem from social factors, and still others represent a synthesis of both acting together. The ways in which these two types of factors might combine to influence human behavior has not been seriously considered by the Gluecks, nor by most other Empiricists, but they seem to be convinced that more than one type of force is at work and that they are not all reducible to the same theoretical framework.[5]

Probably the most thoughtful expression of the Empiricists' basic eclecticism has been offered by Paul Tappan who suggests that:

. . . neither the fact that crime is culturally defined nor the fact that it is biologically and socially normal in an etiological sense should be taken to mean that specific forms of criminal conduct are unrelated to the physical condition or to the hereditary traits of the offender . . . in so far as criminal acts proceed from peculiarities of personality, disposing the individual toward particular lines of conduct, it is reasonable to impute to biology both the foundations out of which such personality variables develop and, *pro tanto,* a role in the criminal behavior that ensues.[6]

Tappan also makes it clear in the same work that he considers certain types of personality disorders as important factors in the etiology of delinquency and crime, i.e., as predisposing the individual toward behavior patterns that are considered illegal by his community.[7]

In proposing a causal role for physiological and psychological forces in human behavior, it should be noted that Tappan is not simply suggesting that eventually everything influences crime and delinquency. To avoid this empty assertion Tappan distinguishes between two types of causes, proximate and essential. Proximate causes are those conditions that contribute to an event even though they are not sufficient to produce it by themselves, while essential causes include those circumstances that alone are sufficient to cause the event.[8] When referring to the role of personality and physiological factors in crime, Tappan is obviously suggesting that they may on occasion act as essential causes. To suggest that they are only proximate causes would say very little, since virtually any kind of factor can contribute to a given pattern of behavior. The search is for essential causes, and Tappan is clearly asserting that nonsocial factors can be essential in bringing about criminal and delinquent behavior.

But if physiological and psychological processes are essentially related to crime, the question still remains, how do strengths and weaknesses at the physiological level, for example, actually influence overt behavior patterns? In answer, Tappan suggests that they probably act both as limiting factors restraining the individual's ability to respond in certain conventional ways and as sensitizing factors rendering the individual particularly responsive to certain kinds of stimuli.[9] Tappan fully accepts the fact that criminality and delinquency are designated as such by the community, but he also feels that in some cases illegal acts may have been caused essentially by personality disorders that in turn may even have been precipitated by constitutional abnormalities. He does not, of course, intend to repudiate social forces as essential causes of crime and delinquency, but he is clearly not satisfied that they are the *only* such causes.

It should be noted that unlike other Empiricists, Tappan fails, explicitly at least, to hypothesize that the several different types of essential causes are all acting in union to bring about deviant behavior. Rather, he seems to imply that the different types of factors are behaving in serial fashion: the physiological system of the individual limiting and focusing his psychological development, which in turn limits and focuses the nature of his social experience. Unlike the Gluecks, for example, Tappan seems to assume that each system of forces remains distinct from the rest in exerting its influence over any particular individual's behavior.

In sum, then, the Empiricists and their rivals, the Purists, through the years have engaged in many skirmishes that have revolved essentially around the significance of nonsocial factors in influencing criminal and delinquent behavior. The Purists have been consistent in their rejection of nonsocial explanations, implying that the essential causes at bottom are all social in nature. The Empiricists, for their part, have not been timid in studying the relationships between delinquency and such nonsocial factors as body build, psychodynamic characteristics, and attitudinal complexes. They have not, however, succeeded in developing an adequate theoretical justification for their many-sided approach to delinquency and crime. Their biggest failure in this regard has been their reluctance to *clarify how forces at several different levels of analysis can combine to determine human behavior.* The Gluecks have demonstrated a passing interest in the problem, and Tappan has confronted it somewhat more directly, but much remains to be done before the eclectic tendencies of the Empiricists become acceptable to the Purists.

This, then, is the nature of the controversy that has separated the Purists and the Empiricists these several years. It has undoubtedly stimulated a heightened concern on the part of the Empiricists for describing delinquency objectively and accurately, and under its impetus the Purists have struggled manfully with some of the problems surrounding the explanation of delinquency. But the conflict has today outlived its usefulness, because theoretical tools are now available for resolving the issues it raises.

An Offer of Mediation

Since delinquency and criminality are clearly types of human behavior, we might expect that a theoretical system with human behavior as its principle focus is best equipped to clarify and resolve the issues that currently divide the Purists and the Empiricists. The theory of social action as recently formulated by Parsons and others represents the most sophisticated attempt thus far to deal comprehensively with human behavior, and consequently it is to this viewpoint that we now appeal.

To begin, let us examine the question as to whether nonsocial factors can act as essential causes of social action. Social action theory is quite definite on this point. It pictures social action as the result of motivational and cognitive systems expressed in normatively regulated ways through social interaction.[10] The theory of social action, therefore, explicitly assumes that psychological forces are relevant to social action and that they do essentially influence the course of behavior. It also recognizes the significance of physiological factors to social action, but here the nature of the relationship is less clearly spelled-out.[11] Thus, social action theory seems to support the contentions of the Empiricists that delinquency should be studied from more than one viewpoint and with more than one theoretical framework.

A second question that social action theory also touches upon is the manner in which several different theoretical viewpoints are to be utilized in explaining delinquency. Although social action theory regards action as the result of four distinct types of forces converging in time and space, it also maintains that each of these systems must be kept analytically distinct, both from each other and from social action itself.[12] Each of these systems, i.e., the physiological, the psychological, the social, and the cultural, displays a logical integrity that forbids its full conceptual integration with other systems at different levels of analysis. Each system, to be sure, affords a certain insight into specific facets of human behavior, but they cannot all be merged into a single coherent theoretical framework.[13] The usefulness of each theoretical system is based upon its logical consistency, and to nullify this by an indiscriminate marriage with alien points of view would simply destroy the original basis for such a union. On this point, social action theory seems to be chastising the Empiricists for combining analytically distinct factors in the explanation of delinquency without clarifying the bases upon which such a combination might be logically undertaken.

Furthermore, the suggestion that four different types of force-systems converge to produce social action implies quite clearly that social action itself must also be kept conceptually distinct from each of the theories used in its analysis. It is much more complicated than any *one* of the theories anticipates, and for this reason its definitive explanation is beyond the scope of any of them, taken individually. It would seem that the Purists particularly have failed to heed this point.

When studying complex patterns of behavior like delinquency and crime, there is a strong temptation to confuse the actual behavior with the theory used in its explanation and to conclude on the basis of this confusion that only concepts at a particular theoretical level can be used legitimately in explaining the behavioral patterns. Thus, once the Purists were satisfied that delinquency is a social fact, the conclusion quickly followed that only social facts should be used in its explanation, and Durkheim's assertion cited previously only served to strengthen their conviction on this point.[14]

Instead of arguing that delinquency is a social fact, however, they might better have argued that the legal standards used to designate delinquency are cultural facts, that the normative patterns of delinquent groups are social facts, and that the emotional patterns underlying the delinquency of individuals are psychological facts.[15] From the standpoint of social action theory, delinquency represents a blending of all these abstract patterns, and to regard any one of them as entirely responsible for the tendencies exhibited in delinquent behavior is a mistake.

On this same point, social action can be likened to a symphonic composition. A symphony, like social action, consists of several different themes that are complexly interwoven to yield an over-all pattern or design. Since no one theme is fully equivalent to the over-all design, neither a symphony nor social action can be analyzed into its parts without losing some of the intricate and coordinated beauty of the integrated pattern. To insist otherwise is seriously to underestimate the complexity of the pattern being studied. This, of course, is not to say that analytic tools should never be used in the study of complex phenomena but that these tools must be coupled with a willingness to appreciate the variety of themes that comprise most empirical phenomena.

A third issue that has also tended to enflame the controversy between the Purists and the Empiricists, but which has been dealt with only obliquely in social action theory, is the failure of both to distinguish between social action as an active, organizing process and social action as a passive, reactive process.[16] On the one hand, social action is viewed as a process whereby man adapts to his environment in an active, dynamic fashion so as to win maximum satisfaction from it, and on the other, it is seen as a socially conditioned process whereby man conforms unselfconsciously and uncritically to the normative pathways of his society. It is no doubt true that both ways of viewing social action describe the behavior of everyone, but it is also true that both ways of interpreting social action must be kept distinct, because they are based on completely different assumptions regarding the manner in which social and psychological factors interrelate to produce social action.

Those who are primarily concerned with action as a passive response to socializing influences, i.e., as socialized action, generally assume a plastic individual that internalizes in a fairly simple and straightforward fashion the narrowing restrictions of his social environment. Their basic problem is to explain why the individual conforms to the pathways of society as closely as he does, and they regard the individual's psychological inclinations as proximate causes of behavior—as providing a kind of motive force, but not as responsible for the specific channels through which action flows. These channels are shaped by social forces, and the individual is molded to them by techniques of socialization and enculturation. Hence, the *essential* causes of social action are all social in nature.

Those who view action as a dynamic process, however, usually adopt a somewhat different position. Their fundamental problem is understanding how the individual through social action is able to engage his situation and use it to the fullest advantage. They are not so much interested in the conditions that generate fairly stable attitudes and orientations in the individual as they are in the forces that influence imaginative, effective decisions. For this reason these theorists are mainly concerned with spelling-out in detail the ways in which particular attitudinal and motivational complexes sensitize the individual to the opportunities of his situation. From their standpoint, a theory of action must provide an understanding of the ways in which the individual's motivational and cognitive systems prompt a utilization of the milieu to his own best advantage. For them the milieu is relatively constant and unchanging, and it is the psychological systems of the individual that are fluid and change-able. Thus, social action from their viewpoint is the result of psychological forces acting as essential causes sifting and selecting alternatives from a relatively stable social environment.

Both of these interpretations of social action are valid, and the questions they raise are fundamental to any explanation of human behavior. Indeed, these same distinctions have taken firm root in sociological theory and each has given rise to a well established theoretical point of view.[17] But a serious difficulty develops as soon as *all* action is regarded as essentially socialized action, i.e., when social action is assumed to be socialized action. Social action theory, of course, recognizes that the behavior of some will not correspond exactly to the normative patterns of their environment; but it also acknowledges that most indi-viduals conform to social patterns much of the time. The concept of socialized action, however, leaves little room for the study of idiosyncratic behavior, and for this reason it is too narrow to serve as a general interpretation of behavior.

It fails as a general concept largely because it as-sumes, first, that the internalized standards guiding behavior correspond closely to the normative stand-ards endorsed by the social environment and, second, that these normative standards are neatly designed to resolve most of the situations encountered by the members of society in their daily rounds.

Both assumptions may be relatively valid for certain individuals, but neither is valid in a general way. In the first place, it is a serious oversimplification to assume that the internalized standards guiding an individual's behavior closely parallel the normative standards of his reference groups. They rarely do, since immediately upon being internalized these standards are subtly molded to harmonize with the existing patterns already within the individual's mind. To be sure, there will be a rough correspondence between the attitudes of most of us and the group's expectations regarding our behavior, but it is important to recognize that this correspondence can only be a rough one, especially where the behavior is deviant. In explaining delinquency, it is necessary to take into account not only the social laws that define the nature of the social structure but also the psychological laws that govern the growth of attitudinal and motivational complexes in the individual. And any systematic attempt to understand social action that fails to do so will prove gross and inadequate.

It would be equally unwise, furthermore, to assume that internalized normative standards are so closely relevant to each of the situations the individual encounters that he can apply them in an uncritical, unreflective fashion. The complexity of most situations that the individual meets beyond early childhood is so great that no amount of socialization or enculturation could equip him with a repertoire of standards sufficient to anticipate every facet of each new situation. The members of groups are forced in most instances to extemporize, that is, to fashion their actions self-consciously out of standards that only crudely approximate the situations at hand.[18] But in consciously fashioning these decisions in this way, the individual is mobilizing affective and unconscious tendencies as much as he is attitudes more or less reflective of social expectations. For these reasons, it would seem that a field theory of behavior similar to that developed by Kurt Lewin would be more appropriate in explaining action generally than a theory based upon these kinds of overly simple assumptions.

Conclusion

The Empiricists have neglected to develop an adequate justification for their assertions regarding the interplay between analytically different force-systems, whereas the Purists for their part have developed an overly narrow explanation of delinquency and crime that tends to confuse the behavior being examined with the abstract sociological concepts used in its analysis and that seriously oversimplifies the ways in which the individual with all his personal abilities and needs engages the normative pathways of his social environment. Naturally, an adequate analysis of delinquent behavior must avoid these mistakes; accordingly, I shall attempt to show in these pages that delinquency, like other forms of social action, reflects the influence of forces at several different levels of abstraction and that in general delinquency is more complex than any single theory used in its analysis. I shall also indicate how theories at different levels of analysis can be combined to explain delinquency without postulating at the same time an amorphous mass of forces combining arbitrarily to shape behavior. Moreover, while indicating the ways in which these theories can interrelate, I shall show that there are three general classes of delinquents defined in terms of the kind of forces that are dominant in their behavior and the structures through which they are expressed.

The aim of this study, then, is to show how several rather distinct developments in social action theory and in the study of delinquency can be integrated in such a way that the basic complexity of delinquent behavior can still be appreciated after it has been analyzed and interpreted in light of a general conceptual framework. The need for such a formulation becomes obvious when the issues that have separated the Purists and the Empiricists are carefully examined. Each viewpoint, however, can provide a valid insight into the nature of delinquency and criminality, and it is our task to reconcile these apparently contradictory viewpoints by means of a framework that encompasses them both.

NOTES

1 Emile Durkheim, *The Rules of the Sociological Method,* 5th ed. (Glencoe: Free Press, 1938), p. 110.

2 Edwin H. Sutherland, and Donald R. Cressey, *Principles of Criminology,* 5th ed. (Philadelphia: Lippincott, 1955), pp. 115, 130, and 135; and Karl F. Schuessler and Donald R. Cressey, "Personality Characteristics of Criminals," *American Journal of Sociology,* Vol. 55, No. 5 (March, 1950), 476–84.

Frank E. Hartung, "A Critique of the Sociological Approach to Crime and Correction," *Law and Contemporary Problems,* XXIII, No. 4 (Autumn, 1958), 703–34.

Michael Hakeem, "A Critique of the Psychiatric Approach," in Joseph S. Roucek, ed., *Juvenile Delinquency* (New York: Philosophical Library, 1958), pp. 79–112.

3 Sheldon and Eleanor Glueck, *Physique and Delinquency* (New York: Harper & Row, 1956), p. 42.

4 Sheldon and Eleanor Glueck, *Family Environment and Delinquency* (Boston: Houghton Mifflin, 1962), p. 9.

5 To be sure, the Gluecks have attempted to describe some of the ways in which these two types of forces interrelate, but at the heart of their analysis is a type of relationship in which the forces at different levels are

"dynamically reciprocal in their influence . . . ," ibid., p. 19. They seem reluctant to abandon a concept of this interrelationship as essentially a confusion of factors.

[6] Paul W. Tappan, *Crime, Justice, and Correction,* (New York: McGraw-Hill, 1960), p. 708.

[7] *Ibid.*, pp. 145–68.

[8] *Ibid.*, pp. 68–69.

[9] *Ibid.*, pp. 103–4.

[10] Talcott Parsons and Edward A. Shils, *Toward a General Theory of Action* (Cambridge, Mass.: Harvard University Press, 1952), pp. 53–54.

[11] Talcott Parsons, "An Approach to Psychological Theory in Terms of the Theory of Action," in Sigmund Koch, ed., *Psychology: A Study of Science,* Vol. 3 (New York: McGraw-Hill, 1959), pp. 647–51.

[12] Talcott Parsons, "Social Structure and the Development of Personality," in B. Kaplan, ed., *Studying Personality Cross-Culturally* (New York: Harper & Row, 1961), pp. 167–68.

[13] On this point social action theory itself is not completely clear. Parsons emphasizes over and over again that the behavioral sciences—sociology, cultural anthropology, psychology, and physiology—are conceptually distinct; but, on the other hand, he also suggests that they can all be integrated into a general theory of action. It would seem, however, that Parsons is not proposing a general *theoretical* framework for the explanation of social action so much as he is suggesting a *strategy* for the analysis of social action. That is to say, he is suggesting how several conceptually distinct theories might be applied in a coordinated way to the problem of social action.

[14] It is worth noting that Durkheim himself was careful to avoid this mistake. Indeed, he seems to acknowledge that behavior as such is a synthesis of several different types of abstract "facts." See especially his footnotes on pp. 103 and 112 in the work cited above.

15 Albert K. Cohen's definition of deviant behavior in which he distinguishes between the implications that institutionalized expectations and personality structures contain for behavior demonstrates the advantages of making the distinctions advocated here. See his "The Study of Social Disorganization and Deviant Behavior," in Robert K. Merton, Leonard Brown, and Leonard S. Cottrell, Jr., eds., *Sociology Today* (New York: Basic Books, 1959), p. 462.

16 Parsons hints at the difference between these two types of action in his suggestion that a distinction must be made between the actor as object and as ego. See his "The Point of View of the Author," in M. Black, ed., *The Social Theories of Talcott Parsons* (Englewood Cliffs: Prentice-Hall, 1961), pp. 324–25.

17 The theory of social action as originally developed by Weber was concerned among other things with explaining how the voluntaristic impulses of the individual can be harnessed to the needs of society; and Lewin, of course, used much the same approach in developing his field theory of behavior. On the other side, symbolic interactionism in the hands of Cooley and Mead has concerned itself primarily with describing the ways in which the individual is molded to his social environment.

18 This was precisely W. I. Thomas' point in his discussion of the Creative, Bohemian, and Philistine types. See his "Three Types of Personality," in C. Wright Mills, ed., *Images of Man* (New York: Braziller, 1960), pp. 406–9.

CHAPTER 2

On Relating Theories at Different Levels of Analysis

The first task confronting those who would provide an adequate explanation of delinquency is that of clarifying the ways in which theories at different levels can be combined to explain social action. We have already seen that there is no longer any reason to dispute *whether* different theoretical structures are relevant to social action, but it still remains to indicate specifically *how* they can be applied to social action.

This problem is somewhat more complicated than it might appear at first glance. The theoretical structures immediately relevant to social action, i.e., sociology, cultural theory, personality theory, and physiology, have themselves been worked out only in a preliminary way. Thus, it is difficult enough to determine the implications of each theory for its own proper phenomena without having also to determine how it is relevant to social action or to the other theories.

This problem will eventually be resolved, but a more troublesome difficulty is contained in the generally accepted notion that these four theoretical points of view are essentially independent of one another. Most theorists today readily admit that although their particular viewpoint is effective in explaining phenomena at a given level of analysis, phenomena at other levels must be explained by other theoretical points of view. Thus, sociologists usually do not presume to suggest to the psychologists that the principles of mental behavior are implicit in the laws that govern society, and most modern psychologists realize that the principles of social organization cannot be inferred from the conscious or unconscious patterns of the human mind. Each theoretical point of view, therefore, presents an integrity of its own that is neither implied by, nor competitive with, the integrity of other theoretical positions.

But if each theoretical point of view is independent of all others, it follows that the manner in which social, cultural, psychological, and physiological forces collectively influence social action cannot be explained or anticipated in terms of a general theoretical structure. If there are no necessary connections between these several different theories, there is no basis for a general theory of their interaction.

In concrete terms this means that nothing in the theory of society or in personality theory determines *unequivocally* how certain social situations and certain personality types shall come together to determine the behavior of specific individuals. From the point of view of both theories, virtually any combination of situations and personality types is permissible. To be sure, there may be some empirical tendency for a particular personality type to seek out a particular situation; e.g., authoritarian types may enter the armed services more frequently than other types because of a congruency between their inner needs and the requirements of military life, but there is no necessary reason why many other kinds of personality types could not also enter the armed forces. Clearly, then, if we assume that sociology, cultural anthropology, psychology, and physiology are all independent disciplines in the sense that the implications contained in one cannot be inferred from the others, it follows that we cannot construct a general, coherent theory of human behavior.

A Strategy for the Analysis of Social Action

But this inability to construct a general theory of behavior need not mean that the study of social action, in general, and of delinquency, in particular, must remain forever an artistic, intuitive endeavor. Although we may not be able to define a closed theory of social action, we can still develop a strategy for the analysis of social action, i.e., an approach to social action that enables us to identify causal relationships quickly and easily.[1] This strategy, however, will be finally determined not by the nature of any particular theoretical system but by the ways in which different kinds of force-systems operating at different levels *can* logically combine to shape social action.

Let me explain. Even though each theoretical discipline is unique and independent of all other disciplines, they all have one thing in common that allows us to speculate about their logical interrelationships: the force-systems that each theory describes can be expressed only through the behavior of concrete individuals. Thus, even though in the abstract the several disciplines are independent, their concrete effects do come together and are reconciled in some fashion in the behavior of individuals. And because the implications of each discipline directly confront those of other disciplines in the individual, it is possible to describe the nature of these confrontations and design a strategy for their analysis.

In practice, this means that insofar as each individual is subjected to more than one kind of force-system, he must, in putting together a reasonably integrated plan of action, find some way of reconciling and reducing the pressures of each force-system to an overarching, coherent pattern. This overarching plan of action expresses, moreover, not only the positive influences that each force-system brings to bear upon the individual but also the limits with which each force-system restricts his behavior. Thus, each discipline not only has a hand in directly shaping the individual's behavior, but it also has a veto over the ways in which *other* force-systems may influence his behavior. Hence, a certain logical consistency is bound to emerge in the manner in which abstract and independent theories interrelate concretely to influence human behavior, and it is, therefore, possible to define a strategy for the analysis of social action.[2]

To illustrate this point, let us consider the following example. From the standpoint of social theory, there is no compelling reason why a society might not entirely proscribe sexual behavior among at least a few of its members. But the society that actually carries out such a policy is certain to find that the sexuality of these members is expressed in many subtle and unusual ways, because, psychologically speaking, sexual needs are not altogether suppressible. Thus, personality theory prescribes certain imperatives regarding behavior that no other theory, including social theory, can violate; and although it carries no implications for social theory itself, personality theory does restrict the ways in which social forces can influence social action. This same argument, of course, applies to all other disciplines that are relevant to social action.

But before we can specify in detail the nature of the logical relationships that exist between two independent disciplines like sociology and psychology, we must first examine several assumptions about the nature of the world that these theoretical disciplines are attempting to explain. To begin, I would suggest that the empirical world consists not of a *single* web of interrelated events but of several families of events unfolding at different levels and that each family, or system, of events proceeds somewhat independently from all the rest. Thus, from this point of view any given, concrete event in reality is made up of several different levels of events and, therefore, can be usefully studied from several different theoretical positions.

Napoleon Bonaparte, for example, was not only an instrument of broad social and political currents in nineteenth century Europe; he was also a personality with unique motivations, energies, and talents; a biological organism with powerful capacities and serious deficiencies; a collection of chemical processes; and an aggregate of atoms. Napoleon's actions were not simply social or political in nature, they were supported by several families of events at different levels, each contributing to the behavior that the historians have identified as Napoleon's. In terms of this first assumption, then, any empirical event consists in reality of several families of events proceeding at different levels and in distinctive ways, but combining so as to give a unique stamp to the empirical event in question.

For our second assumption, I would suggest that these several families of events combine to determine the nature of men like Napoleon in that the more abstract families constitute the environments within which the less abstract events unfold. For example, the environment to which Napoleon's personality was re-acting was the social, economic, and political currents of nineteenth century Europe; and his personality, in turn, formed the environment within which his digestive, circulatory, nervous, and endocrine systems functioned. Thus, each family of events is implicated in a more general system of events, which, in turn, is part of an even more general system of events; until ultimately a comprehensive system is reached. In terms of this assumption, then, the several families of events that constitute human behavior are related to one another in that their respective fates are worked out concentrically, telescoping into one another to define social action.

This way of looking at nature, of course, is an old one that has been endorsed by many scientists and philosophers over the years.[3] One of the more recent endorsements has come from Ludwig von Bertalanffy, who suggests that physical, chemical, and biological systems interrelate to form ". . . a tremendous architecture, in which subordinate systems are united at successive levels into ever higher and larger systems."[4] The basic fact distinguishing one level from another, according to Bertalanffy, is the unique character of the force-system at each level, which, in turn, is largely responsible for the distinctive organizational patterns found at each level.[5] Clearly, he is using the same model of the empirical world as that sketched above.

Now, if the empirical world is viewed in this fashion, it means that our attempts to explain the world theoretically must also exhibit a rather distinctive character. The theoretician is faced with a formidable job in charting the uniformities of a class of events, because in general the class of events in which he is interested will be influenced not only by forces that are peculiar to it as a class but also influenced indirectly by the flow of events at levels immediately adjacent to it. The psychologist, for example, must infer the principles of psychological behavior from motives and images that are confounded to some degree by the patterning of events at both the social and the physiological levels. This problem probably becomes less difficult as the events become more microscopic, but at the level of social behavior it is serious indeed.

Moreover, if the families of events that make up any given event are related concentrically to one another, it also means that their theoretical explanations are arranged hierarchically with respect to one another. Thus, if atoms are typically implicated in chemical processes, which, in turn, are typically involved in biological processes, it means that chemistry as a theoretical discipline assumes the existence of physics and that biology assumes the existence of chemistry. Since chemistry seeks to explain the second-order arrangements of atoms, it is at a higher level than physics; and since biology attempts to understand the second-order arrangement of molecules, it is at a higher level than chemistry; and so on, up to sociology. This is not to suggest that a society is nothing more than a highly complex arrangement of atoms, nor that sociology is in any sense preferable to lower level disciplines, but it is to suggest that there is a hierarchy among the several disciplines defined in terms of the organization of nature.

This way of viewing science helps clarify certain questions about transtheoretical relationships, but it also raises some interesting questions regarding the process of natural evolution. Abraham Edel, for example, suggests that if the sciences are theoretically independent but hierarchically related to one another, it means that events described by higher level theories must assume the existence of events at the lower levels.[6] Thus, the emergence of higher level systems became possible historically only after lower level systems had already achieved a level of maturity. It means, in other words, that the process of evolution in nature consists of two separate but related processes: the maturation of events and systems at each level; and the successive addition of higher level systems as the systems at each level approach maturity.

Edel further suggests that the emergence of these higher level systems may have progressively altered the basic principles describing the behavior of the lower level systems.[7] It is an interesting idea but I doubt very much that the emergence of complex civilizations, for example, has changed fundamentally the principles underlying man's psychological behavior. Civilization may have enabled him to realize more readily his full psychological potential, but it seems unlikely that it has *directly* influenced the very nature of the principles underlying his psychological behavior.[8]

Edel has examined several of the implications that are contained in the point of view presented here, but there is one issue that he fails to clarify, namely, the precise ways in which theoretical structures that are independent can be combined to explain the same series of empirical events. If sociology and psychology describe families of events that unfold at different levels of analysis, how precisely can social and psychological forces unite in individuals to determine social action? How can these independent disciplines be reduced to the same level and focused upon the same problem?

The solution to this difficulty is clearly implied in our second assumption. Families of events functioning at different levels can and do converge to influence the same event, since every event is *both* an element in a broader system of events and an integral system in its own right. Thus, from the viewpoint of sociology each person is an actor participating in a social system of actors, but from the viewpoint of psychology each person is also a complex system of attitudes and motives. Because the individual has this dual nature, he is sensitive to social and psychological pressures, and both sociology and psychology have a parallel, if not a converging, interest in human behavior. This argument, incidentally, is perfectly general, suggesting a common interest in certain problems on the part of all adjacent disciplines.

Three Distinct Types of Social Action

If this way of viewing the problem is valid, it means further that there are only a limited number of ways in which theoretical structures at different levels can be utilized to explain the nature of specific events. Because the integral systems at one level are elements, or units, at the next higher level, the limitations inherent in the nature of the lower level systems will also determine what may *not* happen at the higher level. Thus, a lower level theory, through its ability to fix the limitations of the systems at its own level, also establishes the *range* of possibilities for individuals or units at the next higher level as well.

Suppose, for example, that the laws of psychology set a limit to the amount of stress that human beings can tolerate. Any society that systematically exposes its members to stress beyond these limits will alienate many of its members and be faced with wholesale defections and ultimately with collapse. The theory defining the nature of each individual's personality determines the degree to which he can withstand psychological stress, and every society, regardless of its own immanent tendencies, must respect these psychological limitations. Generally speaking, then, a theory at a lower level restricts the range of patterns that can occur at a superior level by virtue of the limitations this theory places upon the adaptability of its own systems, which in turn also participate as units in the systems at the next higher level. Thus, in this fashion, theories at the lower levels place rigid restrictions on the course of events at the higher levels.

It is also true, however, that the actual patterns taking place at the higher level in their own way influence the course of events at the lower level. The actual pattern of events at any given level is influenced by two distinct sets of conditions: the immanent tendencies specific to that level and the character of the environment to which these tendencies are forced to adapt. But, as we have already suggested, the character of the environment depends to a large extent upon the nature of the higher level systems. Hence, the actual patterns developing at the higher level also exercise an influence upon the course of events at the lower levels, because they are the context within which the lower level events must unfold.

Let me illustrate. The actual nature of the social structure in any given society presents its members with a specific set of normative standards to which each individual must adjust in terms of his own psychological inclinations. Each member of the society

is allowed some latitude in fashioning his life-organi-
zation, but in general, society steers everyone more or
less gently along certain, appropriate lines of behavior. Thus, the social structure presents the individual with a series of values, norms, and customs that
are transformed into attitudes and motives and are
utilized as guides to action. The kinds of images and
emotional patterns that to a considerable extent
dominate the individual's psychological life originate,
therefore, in the structure of his society. It is in this
fashion that the actual patterns unfolding at the higher
level influence the course of events at the lower level
as well.

Now, in many cases it is probably true that the
pressures and limitations of the higher level patterns
do not strain the integrity of the lower level individual
to any great degree, and consequently such individuals
commonly adapt quite easily to the conditions laid
down by the higher level patterns. Occasionally, however, an unusual individual may emerge at the lower
level who in some sense is incompatible with the
higher level patterns. This incompatibility can develop for any number of reasons; for example, it may
be based upon an unusual tendency or need on the
part of the individual, or alternatively, it may be
based upon the individual's unusual integrity.

In the first case, the unit, or individual, at the lower
level may find that he cannot fulfill his basic needs
within the context of the higher level pattern, because
the higher level system has failed to anticipate the
unusual nature of his needs. As a result the lower
level structure or individual may find adjusting to the
environment distressing. Certain types of mental illness illustrate this kind of incompatibility quite nicely,
since they stem from highly unusual cognitive and

motive patterns in the individual that are not compatible with any of the conventional roles society has established for its members. In the throes of an hallucination, the paranoid schizophrenic often seeks to express powerful feelings of revenge in ways that are not permissible in any of the situations in which he customarily finds himself. His own immanent tendencies and the range of opportunities prescribed by his society are in basic conflict.

The second type of incompatibility is based not so much upon a conflict in tendency or need between the two levels as upon a competition regarding which level shall establish the basic organization of the individual's behavior. This type of incompatibility would tend to arise most often when the lower level pattern exhibits an internal unity or coherence that renders it relatively intractable to the shaping pressures of the higher level pattern. In such a conflict the lower level pattern often stubbornly maintains its own intrinsic line of development regardless of the direction encouraged and endorsed by the upper level pattern.

This type of competition is illustrated quite well by the man of true genius who is subjected to considerable stress when his own insights and aspirations fail to coincide in an obvious way with the conventional patterns established by his society. John Maynard Keynes, through a superior understanding of industrial capitalism, recommended that deficit financing was the best way to overcome the stagnation of a severe economic depression. The best economic minds of his day, of course, prescribed exactly the opposite; but Keynes was steadfast in his recommendations, and nearly everyone eventually came to see the wisdom of his viewpoint. He was not mentally or emotionally unbalanced, but his insight into the workings of his environment prompted him to take a deviant position and the integrity of his own personality compelled him to persevere against considerable pressure.

But regardless of the nature of the conflict, it can be shown that there are only three distinct ways in which incompatibilities of this sort can be resolved. First, they can be resolved by modifying the higher level patterns such that the unusual tendencies at the lower level are anticipated and provided for in the structures of the higher level. Thus, if an incompatibility arises between the intrinsic psychological needs of an individual and the social structure of his community, the conflict might be solved by simply establishing a position in the community patterned after the unusual needs felt by the individual.

In general, innovations that are prompted in this way by extraordinary individuals must complement the existing social structure of the community, for otherwise there is an excellent chance that the community will not tolerate the deviancies. Both Billy Mitchell and Martin Luther probably fall within this category, in that both men felt an irrepressible need to reform their respective communities along lines that were consistent with their own predispositions.[9] Both were regarded as mentally unbalanced until the full import of their suggestions was understood and adopted by the society at large. The possibility of resolving basic incompatibilities between the individual and his social milieu in this fashion suggests that the unique individual can at times be a powerful force for social change.

Incompatibilities of this same type can also be found at other levels as well. For example, occasionally an individual's personality may assume an organization that is basically antagonistic to the organization of one of his physiological systems. The psychosomatic reactions that are prompted by this incompatibility will depend upon the nature of the system that is affected, but the basic meaning of these reactions is that there is something wrong, not with the individual's physiological systems but with his psyche.[10] In some cases the incompatibility can be resolved by undertaking a reorganization of the personality so that the needs and limitations of his physiological systems are more carefully integrated into his behavior. Thus, as with the first example, an incompatibility between two levels may be relieved by modifying the structures at a higher level so that they are more consistent with the vital needs of a lower level pattern.

If, however, the pattern at the lower level is extremely unusual, it may not be possible to alter sufficiently the structures at the higher level to make room for the lower level pattern. In this case the incompatibility is truly fundamental, and the only solution may lie in modifying the lower level pattern so that it can behave harmoniously within the framework of the upper level structures. Therefore, when the organization of events at two levels are in *basic* conflict with one another, the higher level pattern can usually be counted upon to prevail in the long run. It must be remembered that the lower level pattern participates in higher level structures as only one member, or unit, among many. It alone cannot reverse or overturn the whole pattern at the higher level, and in a *basic* struggle the single unit, or member, must always lose.

The lower level pattern, however, can itself be reorganized so that its intrinsic tendencies are no longer in conflict with the basic patterns in its environment. If, for example, the lower level pattern happens to be a human personality, the difficulty can be remedied by submitting the individual to psychotherapy and modifying his personality so that antisocial or unconventional motives no longer dominate his social behavior.[11] Or if the incompatibility is between the individual's personality and his physiological system, it can be resolved by administering drugs so that deficiencies in these systems are corrected. Resolving the problem in this manner, however, simply means that the deviant lower level pattern is returned to a more conforming line of development so that basic control over the individual's behavior is returned to the higher level.

In some cases, as I have indicated, the two levels may be entirely irreconcilable, because the integrity of both patterns forbids any kind of compromise. It may be necessary, therefore, to segregate the errant member so that he does not become a dangerous or annoying factor within the larger structure. The criminal, the hopelessly insane, and the mentally retarded must all be isolated when there is no hope of rendering them compatible with society or society compatible with them. And on another plane it is similarly true that some of our physiologically based urges must be ignored or repressed lest the balance of our psyches be endangered; at still another level the body has a whole series of adaptive reactions that function mainly to confine noxious infections to a limited area so that their influence upon the body generally will be minimal. Thus, if nothing else works, the higher level patterns can simply reject the noisome individual and isolate him so that his irritation of the higher level pattern will be kept to a minimum.

All in all, in this brief discussion, we have examined

five ways in which events at two different levels might interrelate with one another. First, we suggested that the ongoing systems at the lower level, because they also enter as units, or individuals, into the higher level, establish rather broad limits that the organization of the upper level system must observe in its own development. Second, when there is a basic compatibility between the structures at two levels, we indicated that the actual patterns exhibited at the lower level depend quite heavily upon the trends unfolding at the higher level. And, finally, when there is a basic incompatibility between the patterns at the two levels, we suggested these three adjustments: the upper level pattern may change so as to accommodate the innovations insisted upon by the lower level structure; the lower level structure may be reorganized so that it can conform to the requirements of the upper level pattern, in which case it simply becomes another example of the second mode above; or the incompatibility can result in a permanent estrangement between the higher and lower level structures.

These five ways in which events at adjacent levels can interrelate, therefore, describe *four* essentially distinct translevel relationships, and of these four types of relationships only three indicate how the *lower level* structures may adapt to the higher level patterns.

There are, therefore, only three distinct ways in which an individual's psychological needs and pressures from his social milieu can interrelate to mold his behavior. (1) If his personal integrity or needs are not highly unusual, his behavior in general will conform to the patterns already established by his social milieu. (2) If his psychological needs are particularly intense or unusual, the impact of his personality may be sufficient to force a reorganization of the structures of his environment; or alternatively, (3) he may become an outcaste and allowed to pursue his basic predispositions only when removed from conventional situations. In other words, the individual can adjust to his social milieu by conforming to it, by reforming it, or by withdrawing from it.

It might help to conceptualize these three basic types of social action by comparing them to the ways in which a mountain stream behaves under varying conditions. Just as the course of human behavior depends upon the ways in which psychological pressures interact with the structure of the social environment, so, too, the path of a stream depends upon the ways in which its own tendencies interact with its channel. Thus, when its banks are high and impervious, the stream has little alternative but to follow its traditional path, dissolving only the minor imperfections that appear in its channel. But when the banks are weak and permeable, the stream's flow may become too powerful for the usual channel, and as a result it may suddenly confront several different possibilities. It may, for example, surge out in an aimless fashion to flood the surrounding country, in which case its path would depend primarily upon the nature of its flow—its velocity and volume—since the restraining influence of the environment is minimal in such situations.

It may also, however, cut a new channel. Initially, the characteristics of the new channel will depend primarily upon the nature of the stream, since the countryside in the beginning is generally receptive to the pressures of the stream. But as a new channel slowly evolves under the action of the stream, its path will gradually be adjusted to the channels above and below the original break; and eventually, the stream will be governed once again by the nature of its channel. Thus, as with human behavior, the stream may either conform to its channel in a rather passive and uncreative fashion, ignoring to a large extent its own spontaneous tendencies; it may burst out of the channel and follow a more or less destructive path that is almost entirely of its own choosing; or it may, through impatience, force major revisions in the channel that ultimately lead to a closer relationship between the inherent capacities of the stream and the structure of its channel. There are here, too, only three alternatives.

Some Conclusions

In this chapter we have sought to lay the foundations for an explanation of delinquent behavior that recognizes its basic complexity and that is not implicitly or explicitly reductionistic. In the first chapter we criticized the Purists for insisting that delinquency is essentially a social phenomenon. We also found fault with the Empiricists for suggesting that delinquency is influenced by many different kinds of forces without indicating how these various forces unite to determine behavior. We have shown here that these mistakes can be avoided and that the alternative to a naïve empiricism need not be a dogmatic oversimplification.

There is still a great deal to be done, however. We have not yet examined the specific psychological and social forces that play an important part in shaping social action, and until we do, it will be impossible to give social action a substantive definition. Nor have we developed a specific set of concepts to describe clearly and easily how the forces behind social action impinge upon the individual and affect his behavior. The battle, in other words, is not yet won.

But we have developed in this chapter a logical structure by means of which a careful explanation of social action in terms of several different kinds of forces might be developed. We have established on the basis of two assumptions regarding the nature of the empirical world that there are only three general types of social action. Two of these types, the reform and the withdrawn types, express the ways in which a personality guided essentially by psychological forces might adjust to a social structure; whereas the third type, a conformistic pattern, describes the adjustment of an individual who is guided more by the strictures of his social milieu than the pressures of his psyche. The first two types describe action that is caused essentially by psychological forces; the third is caused essentially by social forces.[12] Clearly, then, social action includes several basically different types; and as was pointed out in the first chapter, it is important to adopt a view of social action that recognizes this basic variety.

We have attempted here to develop a strategy for the analysis of social action in general and delinquency in particular, and although we have not yet defined the strategy in detail, the assumptions upon which it rests clearly suggest that social action includes only three fundamental types. These types at this point, however, are nothing more than logical categories. To give them a more substantive meaning, we must explore the specific nature of the social and psychological bases of action, and we must examine the ways in which these bases can be used in defining a substantive typology of action and of delinquency. It is to these problems that we now turn.

NOTES

1 Whereas a theory attempts to identify the essential features behind a particular pattern or uniformity in nature, a strategy of analysis seeks to indicate how several patterns can be differentiated from one another so that each can be defined precisely.

2 Logical structures describe the limitations that *all* phenomena must observe in their behavior, whereas theoretical structures describe the *specific* patterns that a phenomena must follow by virtue of its unique and essential nature.

3 See, for example, Edward C. Tolman, "Physiology, Psychology, and Sociology," *Psychological Review*, Vol. 45, No. 3 (May, 1938), pp. 228–41; or S. F. Nadel, *The Foundations of Social Anthropology* (Glencoe: Free Press, 1951), pp. 209–20.

4 Ludwig von Bertalanffy, *Problems of Life* (New York: Harper & Row, Torchbook Editions, 1960), pp. 23–26.

5 *Ibid.*

6 Abraham Edel, "The Concept of Levels in Social Theory," in Llewellyn Gross, ed., *Symposium on Sociological Theory* (New York: Harper & Row, 1959), p. 168.

7 *Ibid.*, p. 169.

8 S. F. Nadel seems to agree on this point. See his *The Foundations of Social Anthropology*, pp. 290–94.

9 See Erik Erikson, *Young Man Luther* (New York: Norton, 1958).

10 These psychosomatic disturbances are nevertheless often mistaken for physiologically based pathologies. Distinguishing the two is not always easy.

[11] The reader will note that the psyche can be out of harmony both with its social environment and its physiological foundations. In the first case, a thorough going reconstruction of the personality is in order whereas in the second a greater openness to certain fundamental urges is indicated. The method used in each case may be roughly similar, but the aims are quite distinct. It is probably true that therapies at other levels, e.g., drug therapy, also display this same bifurcation of function.

[12] See Chapter One, p. 7 and Chapter Three, pp. 67–69 for a detailed discussion of the nature of essential and proximate causes in human behavior.

Three Kinds of Typologies

Ever since Cesare Lombroso published his original analysis of criminality in the nineteenth century, there has been a veritable torrent of typologies reflecting various viewpoints regarding the nature of deviant behavior. Out of all this interest in typologies, however, a precise delimitation of the types of delinquents or criminals that exist has *not* been forthcoming. Instead of the hoped for convergence, we find typologies based upon legal categories, typologies drawn from psychoanalytic theory, typologies based upon sociological theory and physiological factors and typologies derived impressionistically from empirical data. Each of these attempts to capture the essence of crime or delinquency is certainly valid in its own right, but taken together they do *not* provide a progressively finer analysis of deviant behavior. Instead, they present us with a patchwork of typologies that are either incomparable or contradictory.

Our difficulties can probably be traced to some extent to the tendency among some criminologists to deprecate the work of other scholars using different points of view and, thus, to avoid drawing parallels between their respective findings. The problem, however, probably also stems from a more basic failing as well. While criminologists have shown a continuing interest in developing typologies of deviant behavior, they have *not* sought to understand the nature of typologies nor the ways that typologies might (or might not) be utilized in studying deviant behavior.

To be sure, several authors have attempted to provide criteria detailing the manner in which typologies ought to categorize crime or delinquency. Gibbs, for example, suggests that typologies must designate behavioral categories that are homogeneous and similar in etiological development.[1] Gibbons and Garrity feel that typologies should be comprehensive, etiologically based, clear, reliable, precise, and parsimonious.[2] Roebuck thinks that they should consist of "behavioral categories within the confines of legal categories" and that they should show why "certain kinds of people in certain situations commit certain kinds of crimes,"[3] and, finally, McKinney and Kerckhoff have suggested a comprehensive protocol to guide researchers in constructing behavioral typologies.[4] Each of these prescriptions seems reasonable enough on the surface, but unfortunately, none was developed out of a clear understanding of the logic of typologies; and hence, there is no basis other than intuition for accepting or rejecting any of them. In short, it is difficult to tell *why* typologies should be constructed as these authors suggest.

Before we can begin listing the qualities that typologies of delinquency or criminality should possess, it would be well to examine the logical nature of typologies so that we might better appreciate what they are capable of doing. It may turn out that there are several different kinds of typologies, each playing a distinctive methodological role in the analysis of deviant behavior, each constructed in a different way and exhibiting different characteristics.

The Logical Nature of Typologies

In investigating the nature of typologies it is important first to establish exactly what they are and how they differ from other ways of organizing knowledge. A typology consists essentially of a collection of types that are clearly distinguishable from one another but that are sufficiently similar to form a set. The types that constitute a typology are not thrown together arbitrarily; rather, they compose a typology because they are describing the same kind of thing, the same kind of genus, even though they are describing the different forms it can assume.

Typologies, moreover, are generally concerned with patterns that are revealed in the empirical world. There are, of course, many ways of classifying phenomena, e.g., in terms of their grammatical form, in terms of their color, in terms of their geometric shape; but these methods tend to group things together that are only nominally similar, not things that have an essential similarity. Typologies, on the other hand, group things that have something intrinsically in common—genotypically, the members of a type are all one—and their commonality derives from the fact that they all conform to the same scientific laws and develop, therefore, in the same way. Thus, typologies reflect the basic groupings that are inherent in nature itself.

Finally, typologies tend to be concerned with the characteristics that are displayed by acting units, or individuals, not with the relationships among disembodied processes or variables. The several types that constitute a typology describe the ways that individuals, whether they be atoms or human beings, can be structured, with each type reflecting one of the characteristic arrangements that a particular complex of traits can assume. The structure of these complexes varies, of course, from type to type; but collectively, in a typology, they describe the lawful ways that a given set of qualities or factors can be organized in acting individuals.

Generally speaking, the social sciences have made the heaviest use of typologies; perhaps because in the social sciences the unit—the personality, the family, the community, or the society—is much more immediate, and its singularity is much more apparent, than in the physical sciences. The physical scientists, however, have not ignored typologies altogether. The periodic table of elements, for example, has played a very important role in the development of chemistry and physics. But in general the physical sciences have been more interested in the relationships between variables and processes and have not made a heavy use of typologies.

Basically, then, a typology is a collection of types that catalogues the various ways in which a given complex of characteristics can be arranged to explain the behavior of acting units, or individuals. They are bound more by the limitations of nature than by the eccentricities of the human mind, and for this reason they must be constructed within the framework of an empirical science. This does not mean that they must always be drawn *directly* from observation, but it does mean that their basic focus is the empirical universe.

Using this definition of typologies, it is clear that they are something more than a set of classes but something less than a theory.[5] A set of classes can be distinguished from a typology by the fact that classes are generally defined in terms of fewer characteristics. The members of a class have relatively little in common with one another, and accordingly their membership in the same class indicates relatively little about their nature. Males and females, for example, compose two classes, but biological sex alone does not reveal in great detail the nature of the members of either class. Typologies, on the other hand, generally give a much more complete and detailed picture of their members.

Typologies must also be distinguished from theories. The basic function of a theory is to identify the essential forces in nature and to conceptualize these forces so that the implications they contain for each other and for concrete events can be unequivocally determined. Theories are based ultimately on analytic concepts, which are logically interrelated to help explain complex behavior. Typologies, on the other hand, are based on types that describe complex, empirical associations. The orientation of typologies is to the complexity of the empirical world, whereas the orientation of theory is to the analytic simplicity of the conceptual world. A major difference between theories and typologies, therefore, is the object of their concern: for typologies it is the uniformities in nature, but for theories it is the logical relationships that exist between concepts. Typologies strive to clear up and explain the patterns that exist in nature, whereas theories attempt to clarify the implications that inhere in certain basic concepts.

Using these distinctions as our point of departure, it is possible to identify several different ways in which typologies have proved useful in describing the natural world. Indeed, Hempel, the distinguished philosopher of science, has suggested that there are at least three distinct kinds of typologies: classificatory typol-

ogies, extreme typologies, and ideal typologies.[6] A
classificatory typology is the simplest, in that it merely
provides for the classification of cases in terms of
natural, as distinguished from artificial, categories. It
does not specify an ordering of types within the
typology, nor does it confine itself to typical characteristics. It simply defines a series of types that appear to
arrange the empirical universe in significant ways,
without indicating why the types are defined as they
are or which characteristics are essential and which are
not. According to Hempel, Ernst Kretschmer's typology—the aesthetic, pyknic, athletic, dysplastic, and
mixed body types—is a good example of a classificatory typology.

An extreme typology, on the other hand, is one in
which each type is defined in terms of polar characteristics. As with other kinds of typologies, each of the
types describes a complex of characteristics, but with
an extreme typology it is this complex as a whole that
assumes an extreme form. Actual individuals only
rarely conform to the definition of any of the types;
more commonly, they fall somewhere between. Thus,
the polar types are essentially reference points on a
continuum in which the characteristics of one type
gradually shade over into those of the next type.
William Sheldon's typology of mesomorphic, ectomorphic, and endomorphic body types nicely illustrates
this aspect of extreme typologies, since the types themselves are defined as perfect specimens; and the vast
bulk of the population, in effect, are hybrids of two or
more of the pure types.

The main difference between classificatory typologies and extreme typologies is in how the boundaries
between the types are defined. With classificatory typologies, the boundaries delimit qualitative differences

and, hence, are sharply drawn. With extreme typologies, the differences between the types have been reduced to quantitative measurements, and, accordingly, the separation between the types is much less distinct. These two typologies, however, are essentially similar, in that both are based primarily upon empirical observations. Both typologies describe the phenotypic patterns that a given population displays, and their construction is essentially an inductive operation. For this reason, they can be regarded as different versions of a more general kind of typology, which I shall label an *empirical typology*.

Hempel's third typology, an *ideal typology,* is constructed in an entirely different manner. Its types are meaningfully integrated complexes that are derived more or less explicitly from a theoretical structure. As with empirical typologies, they describe the actual patterns that appear in individuals; but in this case, the definition of the types is established in terms of theoretical specifications, and the trait-complexes that constitute each type are meaningfully—logically— interrelated. Hence, the principal function served by ideal typologies is one of systematically drawing together the implications that a given theory contains for acting individuals.

In sum, then, Hempel describes three ways in which typologies have been utilized in the analysis of nature. I have suggested that two of these typologies, the classificatory and the extreme typology, are not essentially distinct and that they should be considered simply as versions of a more general type—the empirical typology. Hempel's third typology, the ideal typology, is obviously distinct from these first two typologies, and accordingly, it has been kept as a separate type. Hempel did not examine the differences between these types in great detail, but an appreciation of their differences is crucial to an understanding of the uses to which these typologies might be put. Let us, therefore, carefully explore the distinctions between these types, and for purposes of convenience we shall consider just the two major kinds of typologies—the empirical and the ideal.

Empirical Typologies

There is no fundamental reason why an empirical typology should not reflect precisely and completely the patterns that exist in nature. With valid and reliable techniques of measurement and with effective methods of inferring uniformities from raw observations, there is no basic obstacle to a perfect reproduction of the regularities that exist in nature in the form of an empirical typology. In practice, of course, things rarely, if ever, approach this degree of perfection. For example, although empirical typologies are defined rather directly in terms of observations, those who have made use of this approach in social science have generally done so with an implicit theory of human nature in mind. Consequently, the resultant typology almost always reflects certain ill-defined assumptions regarding the causes of behavior. This bias means essentially that the researcher will be particularly attentive to certain trends in his data but peculiarly blind to others. Thus, the final version of the typology usually includes a narrower range of types than actually exists, and the types that are included are defined selectively in terms of those characteristics that are relevant to the observer's point of view. Empirical typologies, therefore, are most generally neither comprehensive nor definitive.

Their heavy dependency upon measurement and observation means, moreover, that empirical typologies will tend to focus upon rather concrete characteristics—those that are most amenable to reliable observation. Thus, physiologically based characteristics, like physiognomy and body structure, and the more obvious psychological dimensions, like personality traits, have inspired the definition of many empirical typologies of delinquency or criminality; whereas more elusive characteristics, like the individual's ego-identity or his specific cultural loyalties, have served much less frequently in the definition of empirical typologies. Empirical typologies, therefore, tend to begin with the most obvious patterns, and they move to the more subtle patterns only as suitable methodologies become available.

There are several excellent examples of empirical typologies in the literature on deviant behavior. Lombroso, along with many others in the latter half of the nineteenth century, was convinced that criminality stems primarily from physiological deficiencies; and on the basis of this assumption, he was able to identify five criminal patterns: the born criminal, the epileptic criminal, the moral imbecile, the criminaloid type, and the impetuous and impassioned criminal.[7] It is to Lombroso's credit that he did not simply discard those portions of his data that failed to correspond exactly with his preconceived notions regarding the nature of criminals. When he found that certain criminals did not seem to display any physiological weaknesses, he defined two miscellaneous categories: the involuntary criminal, i.e., the innocent victim of an abstract and highly technical code, whose crime is more offensive to the letter than to the spirit of the law; and the habitual criminal, whose criminality stems from his socialization in crime through a prolonged contact with criminal strata in society.[8]

Lombroso's empirical typology seems to fit the essentials of our earlier sketch quite nicely: (1) his typology is not exhaustive, since it fails to anticipate certain types of criminality that are linked indirectly with psychotic illness; (2) the types that are identified are selective and incomplete; and (3) the focus of the typology could hardly be more concrete in nature—it describes gross physical and behavioral abnormalities.

More recently, Hewitt and Jenkins have also constructed an empirical typology of deviant behavior based upon their observations of several hundred cases at a child-guidance center.[9] The point of view used by Hewitt and Jenkins was psychiatric in nature, and consequently, they described types that focus upon the control and release of basic impulses. The unsocialized, aggressive child, for example, is characterized by an extreme degree of acting-out; whereas the over-inhibited child, as the name implies, is plagued with a painful shyness that prevents most kinds of useful social intercourse. A third type, the socialized delinquent, was defined as a miscellaneous category to include all those delinquents that could not be reasonably fitted into the two psychologically oriented types. Thus, like Lombroso, these authors have formulated a rather limited empirical typology; the types they have described are only sketchily filled-in; a miscellaneous category is provided to take care of the overflow; and the characteristics that form the basis of the types are rather concrete, though certainly less so than Lombroso's.

In general, then, empirical typologies tend to fall into an easily identified pattern. They are not exhaustive in either an extensive or an intensive sense, and they are forced by their very nature to deal with highly concrete kinds of observations. If the observations happen to be quantified, the types themselves may represent polar positions on several continua; if they are not, the types will generally be sharply differentiated from one another in terms of qualitative distinctions. Empirical typologies may make some use of theoretical insights but often in a primitive and even subliminal way. Their principal function is that of charting the actual patterns displayed by specific kinds of individuals. They provide the raw material, as it were, out of which theories are constructed and perfected.

Ideal Typologies

Ideal typologies are also found in abundance in the criminologic literature. For example, Reiss has defined three types of delinquents in terms of psychoanalytic theory: the relatively integrated delinquent, the delinquent with weak ego controls, and the delinquent with defective super ego controls; Sanford has defined three types of criminals in terms of the interrelationships between their id, ego, and superego. Friedlander has identified eight types of delinquents in terms of three pathological processes; and Alexander and Staub have analyzed criminality in terms of the interplay between the conscious and unconscious processes of the mind.[10] As with empirical typologies, when we examine this kind of typology carefully, several distinctive features emerge.

Perhaps the most important feature of an ideal typology is the manner in which it is formulated. It is defined in terms of the implications that a particular theory contains for a specific pattern of behavior, and from this fact both its major strengths and its principal weaknesses flow. Thus, because an ideal typology is grounded in theory, it can often provide considerable insight into the forces behind certain patterns in nature. It can advance, for example, sound arguments to explain why a given individual acts as he does. But, by the same token, because it is derived from theory, it can only be defined if a given theory contains implications for individuals and if these implications form a trait-complex.

There must be, in other words, good theoretical reasons why a particular set of characteristics comes together to form a type. Thus, because sociological theory contains implications for individuals, it should be possible to define a social typology of delinquency in terms of the adolescent roles and cultural traditions that are found in certain kinds of communities and social classes. And similarly, personality theory should also yield an ideal typology of delinquency, because it postulates a complex of attitudes and motives arising out of certain kinds of unconscious conflicts. In principle, it should also be possible to construct a typology of delinquency in terms of legal categories, but the theory explaining the legal code is especially incomplete; and, to attempt to develop a legal typology at this particular time might well be premature. Finally, although it may be possible to define a typology of delinquent behavior in terms of physiological theory, this cannot be attempted here. Thus, it is reasonable to anticipate as many ideal typologies of behavior as there are theories of behavior, although for several reasons we cannot in this essay consider them all.

The theoretical origins of ideal typologies also contain some rather specific implications regarding the nature of ideal typologies. For example, because they are theoretically derived, the types of an ideal typology must be analytically distinct and mutually exclusive; they must be described in terms of characteristics uniformly at the same level of analysis; and collectively, the types should exhaust the full range of patterns that are possible at their level.

Because the types are defined deductively from theory, they tend to assume an all-or-none form, that is, they describe the effect of a factor that is assumed to be either present or absent. Those types that assume the presence of a particular factor are sharply differentiated from those that do not, and since each type is essentially different in at least one way from all other types, every type in an ideal typology is qualitatively distinct from all the rest. Moreover, if the theory upon which the typology is based is closed—if its own foundations have been completely analyzed and their implications thoroughly understood—the resultant typology should include all the types that *can* exist at that particular level.

If the theory is closed, it means that the essential nature of a particular sector of the empirical universe has been fathomed and understood. Any such theory, therefore, should yield a typology that is similarly complete; and since every theory is potentially, if not actually, closed, ideal typologies can in principle include all of the types that occur at their own particular level. And because they must describe these types in terms of dimensions that are at least implicit in their parental theories, the types of an ideal typology must all be defined at the same level of analysis.

It should not be assumed, moreover, that because an ideal typology is exhaustive at its own level of analysis, it can also be exhaustive of the full range of empirical possibilities. On the contrary, because it cannot describe the types that are implied by theories at other levels of analysis, it will not in general be comprehensive at the concrete level. The concrete behavior of individuals reflects the influence of force-systems at several different levels, and since no ideal typology can describe the patterns induced by all of these different forces, it cannot be empirically exhaustive.

But if it cannot be comprehensive, it cannot be intensive either. If, as we have already assumed, human behavior represents the influence of several different force-systems interwoven together, no ideal typology will ever be able to describe its manifold character completely. If, however, it cannot describe concrete behavior completely, it cannot be definitive with regard to any specific behavioral pattern. It is in this sense, then, that ideal typologies cannot be intensive.

To sum up, an ideal typology is mainly a theoretical tool, and it must be evaluated in this light. It cannot anticipate the complexity of the natural world, because it begins from only one set of assumptions. Actual individuals are influenced simultaneously by several different kinds of forces, and accordingly, their resulting behavior is considerably more complex than any single ideal typology can anticipate. The main value of ideal typologies lies in their ability to suggest explanations for specific patterns that appear in behavior, not in their ability to describe precisely what exists. Their function is diagnostic, not cartographic.

Clearly, then, ideal typologies and empirical typologies are basically different, and they should never be confused. Although both usually represent the empirical world only incompletely, empirical typologies can, and occasionally do, approach completeness somewhat more closely than ideal typologies. The main purpose of empirical typologies is to discover the uniformities that nature contains, but they are in no position to do what ideal typologies do, namely, to suggest or identify reasons behind these patterns. These two kinds of typologies are serving quite different functions, and it is very important to keep them distinct when developing standards that each must conform to.[11]

Synthetic Typologies

Neither of these typologies, however, is fully adequate to the complexity of the real world. Ideal typologies can only suggest explanations from one point of view, and empirical typologies are often biased in their description of what exists. For these reasons we must turn to a third kind of typology as yet discussed only implicitly in the social psychological literature.[12]

A *synthetic typology,* as I shall label it, serves mainly to coordinate the implications that each ideal typology contains for a given behavioral pattern so that a comprehensive, coherent explanation of the pattern can emerge. Thus, assuming that delinquency is influenced both by psychological and social forces, a synthetic typology of delinquency would describe the behavior of individuals with typical personality styles in typical social situations. By examining systematically the personality types that psychological theory suggests in terms of certain common social situations, it should be possible to construct a synthetic typology that coordinates the insights of both points of view in the explanation of delinquency. Thus, by articulating the types of those ideal typologies that are relevant to a particular concrete pattern of behavior, it should be possible to provide a balanced and thorough explanation of the pattern.[13]

Synthetic typologies constructed in this fashion will differ in several important respects from the simpler, ideal typologies upon which they are based. First, they will be considerably more complex, and the types within the typology will be considerably less distinctive than with ideal typologies. Their complexity derives from the fact that the types are described in terms of characteristics at several different levels of analysis—all of which must be kept in mind if the type is to be identified properly. This complexity means further that the discrete nature of the types, so marked in ideal typologies, will be less prominent here. The different types in a synthetic typology will share some characteristics, and even though the types will still be readily distinguishable by the trained observer, the boundaries between them will be less sharp than in an ideal typology.

Second, the accuracy and thoroughness with which the types describe actual individuals should be considerably greater than with an ideal typology. The complexity of the synthetic typology, while tending to make it unwieldy, nevertheless enables it to describe more intensively the manifold nature of individuals, because its complexity approximates their own—individuals are also shaped by the forces operating at several different levels of abstraction.

Third, a synthetic typology should embrace a substantially larger portion of the natural universe. Indeed, it should be possible to construct a synthetic typology that exhausts the entire range of patterns that are found empirically in a given problem area. Since all the relevant theoretical levels are utilized in defining a synthetic typology, all the patterns that are possible at *each level* are represented in its definition. In other words, if the ideal typologies upon which the synthetic typology is based are complete, the resultant synthetic typology should anticipate all the types that *can* exist.

Finally, although the complexity of a synthetic typology may improve its precision in classifying concrete individuals, it does not contribute to its applicability. Since some types share certain characteristics, there is every likelihood that some individuals will resemble more than one type and be very difficult to classify. Furthermore, because the number of types included in a carefully constructed synthetic typology may be at least several hundred, specialists may find it difficult to master the entire typology. The advantages of precision and comprehensiveness in this instance are counterbalanced by a burgeoning complexity that hampers the practical administration of such a typology.

This problem, however, has been faced by other disciplines and solved quite satisfactorily. The medical profession, in particular, is confronted with a typology of disease that includes several hundred distinct symptom patterns. It has not, however, responded by shrinking from the resulting complexity and settling for simpler classifying techniques. Instead, individual researchers have been encouraged to confine their efforts to a *sector* of the total disease typology. This may be the appropriate response for those social psychologists who are interested in developing a synthetic typology of certain aspects of behavior.

The Construction of Synthetic Typologies

We have examined the differences between synthetic, ideal, and empirical typologies, but we have failed thus far to consider the most crucial question of all, namely, the precise manner in which several ideal typologies are to be combined to form a synthetic typology. We have suggested up to now that a synthetic typology of delinquency might be constructed by examining the personality types that psychological theory suggests underlie deviant behavior, in the context of each of the social situations that social theory indicates is also relevant to deviant behavior. Thus, a synthetic typology of delinquency could be developed on the basis of the two ideal typologies that are directly relevant to the same problem.

But in order to indicate exactly how these ideal typologies can be integrated to form a synthetic typology, it is not enough to suggest that they be combined systematically. We must still develop a set of concepts that allows us to indicate in concise and accurate terms how forces at several different levels impinge upon acting individuals and influence their behavior. We need, in other words, a set of concepts relevant primarily to behavior and *not* to any particular theoretical viewpoint, but at the same time conceptually consistent with the abstract force-systems that do shape behavior. In short, we need a bridge between the abstract theories that analyze behavior into its essentials and the actual processes that are behind behavior in the concrete. As we have already seen, such a bridge cannot itself become a theory—the theories upon which it is based are independent of one another—but it is nonetheless indispensable to any attempt to develop a full understanding of a specific pattern of behavior.

Fortunately, we already have such a conceptual bridge in Lewin's field theory of behavior. Lewin saw that the explanation of behavior necessarily requires a set of concepts that are specific to the acting individual and not to his psychological or social nature. He clearly understood, furthermore, that the principal function of these concepts is to permit a precise description of the decision processes that are immediately prior to the action. These concepts, as Lewin developed them, are implicated in the psychological system of the individual and, therefore, are quite sensitive to the ebb and flow of a wide variety of psychological forces, but they are not an integral part of psychological theory.

They are, instead, specific to the individual and to the manner in which he organizes a plan of action. Thus, they are not so useful in explaining *why* an individual behaves as he does as they are in identifying *how* he behaves as he does. It would seem that Lewin was quite right when he observed that field theory is more nearly a methodology, or a strategy for the analysis of behavior than it is a theory of behavior.[14]

Two concepts that stand at the heart of field theory illustrate its action orientation quite nicely. The life-space and its more general analogue, the psychological field, refer essentially to the individual's interpretation of his environment as filtered through his cognitive and motivational structures at the moment of action.[15] The events described by these concepts are quite sensitive to psychological pressures of all kinds, since the ways in which the environment is perceived and integrated must conform to psychological laws and principles. These concepts, however, refer to the results of perceptual and cognitive processes and not to the actual forces themselves. Moreover, they also acknowledge the possibility of nonpsychological, as well as psychological factors affecting the course of behavior. Thus, it is clear that Lewin intended these particular concepts, and the larger field theory from which they spring, to serve as a conceptual framework whereby abstract force-systems of several different types—social and physiological, as well as psychological—could be reduced to the same level and utilized in explaining the path followed by the acting individual. Field theory, as such, says very little about the nature of these force-systems and, therefore, has little to add to the theoretical structures that are utilized in explaining behavior. Its main concern is with action and not with the development of theories about the essential components of action.

But because the main focus of Lewin's field theory is upon action, it is also essential to the construction of synthetic typologies of action. To be sure, Lewin himself never attempted a formal typology of action, but field theory lends itself quite readily to this end. Indeed, most of the concepts that Lewin developed originally can be adapted to our own purposes here with little or no modification. Our main attention at this point, however, shall be focused primarily upon four basic concepts, namely, the life-space, the psychological field, the situation, and the social field.

As I have already indicated, there is very little difference in the way in which Lewin used the concepts—the life-space and the psychological field. They both describe the individual's mental image of his situation relative to his momentary needs and fears.

But in conceiving of the psychological field in this fashion, Lewin seems to have departed to some extent from the usual concept of a field. In the physical sciences a field is generally considered to be an area, or region, through which a specific kind of force-system is playing. A magnetic field is a region in which magnetic lines of force are active, and a gravitational field is the space within which the force of a body's gravity is at work. As Lewin used the term, however, a psychological field refers to the over-all *effect* that is produced by certain kinds of forces and not to the space within which these forces operate.

But since it is important to distinguish between the site wherein forces are active and the effects they produce—between the field and its results—we shall draw a clear distinction between the psychological field and the life-space in the following fashion. We shall continue to use the concept, the life-space, as Lewin did to refer to the actual picture the individual has of himself and his surroundings; but following the physical scientists, we shall redefine the psychological field to refer to the space, or region, within which psychological forces are active.

It will certainly include all those conscious, i.e., perceptual and cognitive, processes that are so important in giving the life-space structure, but it will also include those unconscious processes that are only dimly felt in the life-space. Moreover, whereas the life-space reflects the influence of many nonpsychological forces—cultural values and physiological drives—as well as psychological forces, the psychological field describes the domain wherein *only* psychological forces hold sway.

The psychological field, then, refers exclusively to processes and forces of a psychological nature and to the extent of their influence. It is, therefore, a psychological concept with psychological dimensions. The life-space, on the other hand, refers to the mental picture that the individual has of his surroundings, and although it is influenced—sometimes rather strongly—by forces active within the psychological field, its basic function is to represent the processes of *action*. Hence, it is a concrete term describing the actual flow of events in the individual's mind as he contemplates and carries out action.

A similar distinction might also be drawn between the social field and the situation. Just as the psychological field refers to the domain of psychological forces, so too the social field can be defined as the region within which social forces are operative. And the situation might be defined to parallel the life-space as the specific setting wherein social forces particularly (but other kinds of forces, too) converge to give a distinctive structure to the conditions of action. Thus, both the life-space and the situation are pervasively influenced by a particular kind of force-system. But since both refer to concrete phenomena, they also reflect the influence of other kinds of forces as well. Moreover, there is probably a close causal connection between the life-space and the situation, since the life-space in many ways is simply a subjective version of the situation and since the situation also assumes in subtle ways the character of its constituent life-spaces.[16] They are, therefore, paired concepts, reflecting in their own definition the essentially dual character of action as both a subjective and an objective process.

They differ in one very important way, however. Although the life-space is influenced by many different kinds of forces, it can only assume a structure that is consistent with the organization of psychological systems; and, by the same token, the situation can only assume a structure that is consistent with the organization of social systems—although again, many different kinds of forces can and do affect it. Thus, while the life-space and the situation are intimately interrelated, they are also governed by quite distinct principles of organization.

This complex relationship between the two means that as one adjusts in terms of its own immanent needs, it threatens the stability and integration of the other. That is to say, as the individual attempts to organize his life-space in terms of the principles guiding cognitive processes, he may also find that he is increasingly thrown out of harmony with his situation, because it is organized in terms of social principles. If he persists, however, in attempting to regularize his life-space and if the potential structure of his life-space is not too antithetical to the situation, before long the adjustments in his life-space will also be reflected in changes in his situation. Thus, as some individuals attempt to perfect their life-spaces, they may also trigger broad changes within the larger social system. And, by the same token, as the situation attempts to arrange itself in terms of the principles of social organization, it simultaneously imposes new structures and images upon the life-spaces of those involved. Thus, as both the life-space and the situation adapt to the prevailing forces in their particular fields, they also tend to create pressures for change and realignment in the other as well. The life-space and the situation, therefore, are related to one another as partners engaged in a restless dialectic whose rhythms are both a cause and an effect of social and psychological evolution.

I have attempted here to show how Lewin's field theory can be used as a framework within which forces at different levels of abstraction might be logically integrated in the explanation of social action. I have also indicated that this requires essentially two distinct sets of concepts. The first refers to the realm of the abstract and recognizes the existence of only one kind of force or process. The concepts in this set—the social and psychological fields—are analytic in the sense that they help us to think clearly and precisely about the implications that man's social and psychological nature contain for his behavior. They do not indicate the specific mechanisms whereby certain facets of man's nature actually exert an influence upon his behavior, but they do allow us to speculate quite precisely about the limitations and imperatives that psychological and social beings must obey.

The second set refers to the specific mechanisms whereby abstract force-systems actually do impinge upon human beings and mold their behavior in certain ways. They are the windows through which the force-systems described by abstract theories enter the realm of the concrete, confront one another, and ultimately have an influence upon the current of history. Because they deal with the concrete, I shall describe these terms as synthetic.

We have already commented on the complex relationships that the synthetic terms display among themselves, but it is also true that each of the synthetic terms displays, if not an homology, at least a special relationship to one of the terms in the analytic set. Thus, the life-space is organized in terms of psychological principles, and it is particularly responsive to psychological forces. In addition, the situation is organized in terms of social laws and principles and is especially sensitive to social forces of all kinds.

Each of these concrete factors or sites is influenced by other forces, too, but before it can acknowledge these "alien" forces, they must be translated into the genre of the prevailing force-field. Thus, cultural values cannot register within the life-space until they have also become attitudes, and attitudes can have no influence upon the situation until they have been adopted as normative standards either for emulation or attack. Each of these sites, therefore, is under the immediate influence of a single force-field, and although under certain circumstances it may reflect the indirect influence of other fields more strongly than that of its own proper force-field, its structure must be consistent with the range of patterns that are permissible in its own particular force-field. In this sense, then, each of the synthetic terms exhibits a special relationship to one of the terms in the analytic set.

These two sets of concepts suggest many provocative hypotheses. However, we have studied them with one specific purpose in mind: to develop a logical structure whereby a synthetic typology of social action might be constructed. Let us proceed to this task now.

Since the life-space is the immediate basis of social action, our task in essence is that of determining how social and psychological forces can combine to structure the life-space. Because the life-space is especially responsive to the psychological field, it should not be difficult to determine the manner in which psychological forces impart a distinctive pattern to the life-space. Personality theory, which is concerned primarily with the ways in which psychological complexes develop, should prove to be a fruitful source of just such patterns.

The influence that social forces have upon the life-space, however, is somewhat less obvious. Although the social field structures the situation directly, it does not extend into the life-space, and for this reason its influence upon social action must necessarily be somewhat less direct than that of the psychological field. It is still true, however, that images of the situation do enter the individual's life-space and influence the organization that emerges there. The individual uses his perceptions as guidelines for behavior—they enter his life-space as stimuli—and if these perceptions are originally structured in terms of social forces, which is the case when the individual is in a social situation, its structure will be reproduced, after a fashion, within the individual's life-space. The influence of the social field upon social action, therefore, is mediated by *both* the situation and the life-space.

The image of the situation that finally finds its way into the life-space will not ordinarily reflect the situation precisely as it is, since in general it is modified immediately and continuously to blend with images that already exist within the life-space. But insofar as these socially patterned images play a part in shaping the life-space, they must be represented in a synthetic typology of social action.

In defining the influence of social forces upon the life-space, we seem to be confronting two distinct problems. First, we must establish the typical ways in which the situation can be organized, and, second, we must determine how socially patterned images are modified within the life-space to conform to the mental structures already there. The first problem can be

handled quite easily by appealing to social theory as it
applies to the situation and by developing on this
basis a typology of social situations. The latter problem, however, is apparently somewhat more difficult to
solve. Gestalt psychologists have sought for many years
to establish how perceptions adapt to mental images
already present in the mind, but so far they have
made little headway beyond simply charting the distortions that perceptions undergo in different contexts.
Unfortunately, the principles behind these distortions
have not yet been reduced to anything like a systematic
theory.

In Chapter Two, however, we did suggest three
general ways in which social and psychological forces
can interrelate to influence behavior, and these same
general types of social action are directly relevant to
the present discussion.[17] Thus, when an individual's
image of a situation succeeds in dominating his life-
space, his behavior in general will conform rather
closely to the patterns prescribed by his social field;
and even though they are only indirectly influential
in his behavior, the essential causes of his behavior
will all be social in nature. Moreover, the fact that his
life-space is organized basically in terms of social
structures may well mean that the forces in his psychological field are muted and only ineffectively expressed in his behavior. Thus, a strict conformity to
the demands of his environment may force the individual to deny some of the basic wishes implicit
within his own psychological nature and to repress
them into unconsciousness.[18] Such individuals are
usually not completely estranged from themselves, but
their psychological needs enter their life-spaces as
alien forces, triggering behavior that then proceeds
only along highly conventional paths. Curiously

enough, with such individuals, psychological forces function only as proximate causes of their behavior.[19]

Frequently, however, the dominant pressures in an individual's psychological field are not entirely antithetical to the structure of his situation; and when this is the case, he may find that he can freely give expression in social action to many of his most basic psychological needs. In such cases his action will be reformistic in nature, i.e., it will be focused upon imperfections in the situation with a view to reforming them so that they may agree more nearly with the psychological patterns implicit in the individual's life-space. The behavior of these individuals will reflect pressures arising in their psychological fields somewhat more clearly than with the conformistic type, and their personalities will tend to be somewhat more distinct. When they are in a reforming mood, their behavior is guided by patterns prompted by forces within their psychological fields, although at most other times they will generally be content to conform rather peaceably to conventional social patterns. Thus, reformistic action as such is determined essentially by psychological forces, although the reformer ordinarily conforms to most social structures that are not directly relevant to his reforming activity.

Occasionally, the dominant tendencies in the individual's psychological field will be so intense that they cannot be repressed in favor of socially defined structures, while at the same time they are so antagonistic to these structures that there is no basis for a smooth integration with them. Under these conditions the action that results will tend to be isolative, or withdrawn, in character; and although the individual may pay a fearful price for his idiosyncrasies, his life-space will be structured essentially in terms of forces within his own psychological field. Hence, he will rarely do anything that is not motivated and directed by his own psychological needs.

Altogether, then, there are just three ways in which social and psychological fields can interrelate to shape the life-space; and, therefore, there are just three major classes of social action. The three types can be distinguished by the nature of the forces that are responsible for the dominant organization of the life-space and by how the other factors enter and influence the life-space. (1) With the conformistic type, the life-space is organized in terms of social forces, and pressures from the psychological field tend to play a disruptive or, at best, an irrelevant role vis-à-vis the life-space. (2) Reformistic action, however, results when the life-space is organized basically in terms of psychological pressures, and the structure of the social situation serves as a medium through which the emerging patterns in the life-space can be expressed and fulfilled. (3) The withdrawn, or isolative, type of action corresponds to a life-space that is structured basically in terms of psychological forces and that experiences the social milieu as essentially antagonistic and repressive toward its own basic pattern of integration.

These three types of action, then, represent the basic variations that can be written on the theme of behavior, and as such they must be recognized and explained by a synthetic typology of delinquency. We have not yet advanced a detailed and specific discussion of any of these types, largely because we have not yet defined the ideal typologies from which such a discussion might develop. But before we can move to these complex problems, I must point out several basic facts about synthetic typologies.

In using synthetic typologies, it is important to remember that they are an *analytic* tool and, therefore, can never perfectly describe the long-term behavior of any particular individual, since over a period of time most individuals will certainly react to different situations in all three of the ways described above. Thus, a given individual may behave conformistically in his occupation, reformistically in his political behavior, and withdrawn in his relations with the opposite sex. As the situation shifts, we must anticipate that in general the individual will also change the way in which he adapts, and for this reason no single analysis will be sufficient to account for the long-term direction of his behavior.

Moreover, it should be made clear that any given pattern of behavior through time can also be expected to change its basic nature. For example, a pattern of behavior that initially was clearly reformistic, e.g., Keynesian economics, will generally become conformistic as it falls into a routine and becomes an established part of a group's structure. The distinctive feature about social action is not the actual content of the behavior but rather the manner or style in which it is performed. Each type of action exhibits a distinctive style, and everyone shifts among these styles in a more or less flexible fashion. Some individuals may demonstrate a preference for one style over another, but in general as they move from one situation to another, individuals should display considerable variety in the manner with which they behave and relate to their environment. Social action is every bit as dependent upon the situation as it is upon the life-space for its definition.

Summary and Conclusion

We have in this chapter identified three distinct ways in which typologies might be utilized in the study of social action in general and of juvenile delinquency in particular. The ideal typology, we have seen, is mainly useful in summarizing and clarifying the implications that a particular theoretical structure contains for delinquent behavior. It does not pretend to give an intensive picture of any particular offender nor a comprehensive view of the delinquent population as a whole. Its usefulness lies in its ability to clarify and identify the relationship between a specific field of forces and delinquent action.

In a certain sense an empirical typology resembles an ideal typology viewed dimly and from a distance. It is based principally upon observation, but it is also developed in terms of a vague theoretical perspective, since the researcher often sees only those aspects of the world that he is ready to see. It is, nevertheless, an integral step in the construction of a synthetic typology, for it is by means of empirical typologies that the theoretical bases of ideal typologies are clarified and perfected.

A synthetic typology, which is the ultimate goal of those who are interested in crime and delinquency, will be most helpful in providing a complete description of each and every delinquent type that can exist. Its major focus is upon the delinquent population, but its utility derives from the fact that it represents a careful synthesis of the insights into delinquency contained in each of the relevant theoretical structures. Its construction entails a monumental effort, and its practical application will require the skill and experience of a diagnostic physician. It is, however, the foundation upon which an effective treatment, re-habilitation, or prevention program must be based.[20]

Each of these different kinds of typologies, then, serves a distinctive purpose, and each presents a distinctive set of characteristics. There is, also, a definite logic underlying their evolution. The adequacy of a synthetic typology ultimately depends upon the quality of the ideal typologies from which it is constructed. But these can only be as good as the theories from which they are derived, which in turn depend in the last analysis upon the validity of the empirical typologies that are available. Thus, the development of the theories and typologies that are relevant to a given problem-area must proceed in an integrated and balanced way. The first step in the analysis of delinquency, for example, must be an identification of those uniformities in the delinquent universe that are apparent to the relatively unsophisticated observer. Once these have been definitely established, the next step involves the development of a vocabulary that will enable a careful and succinct description of these uniformities. Then, the formulation of a set of concepts to describe these uniformities is a straight-forward operation.

The adequacy of the conceptual vocabulary that is ultimately developed, therefore, depends upon the validity of the initial attempts to analyze the delinquent population into a meaningful typology. If the original types are basically irrelevant to delinquency, the vocabulary will only impede the study of delinquency. But if the initial typology is sound, the vocabulary will yield a fruitful exploration of the problem. Unfortunately, there is no sure way to distinguish before hand a heuristic analysis from one that is essentially irrelevant to the problem. Every researcher is no doubt convinced that his own analysis is sound. But the only proof of his intuitions is in their results. If his intuitions are to the point, his studies will proceed along a path that is rich and rewarding; but if they are misguided, his studies will be encumbered with a terminology that is irrelevant to his subject matter, and his investigations will flounder.

Clearly, then, the formulation of an empirical typology that accurately reflects the patterns of delinquency is an integral step in the definition of a set of basic concepts that describe the problem validly and concisely. Once the basic concepts have been identified and sharpened, the researcher must formulate a set of educated guesses as to why the uniformities that characterize the delinquent population take the form they do. He must begin to develop a set of hypothetical constructs that *explain* the nature of the categories he has defined, and he must organize these constructs into a coherent theory.

The theory, however, at this point is inevitably incomplete, and to bring it to a high level of refinement, it must be compared thoroughly and carefully with the original empirical typologies from which it sprang. Through this comparison the theory can be revised and extended to comprehend every facet of the empirical typology, and under the prodding of theory the typology itself will also be further resolved.

The manner in which a dialogue between an empirical typology and its theoretical base can lead to a gradual refinement of both is nicely illustrated in the physical sciences by the periodic table of elements and its role in the development of atomic theory. The ancients devised a rather simple classification of the elements that made some rather obvious distinctions between fire, water, air, and earth. This scheme prevailed until a more sophisticated view of the universe began to emerge in the seventeenth and eighteenth centuries. As chemical analysis grew progressively more sophisticated, it soon became evident that fire, water, air, and earth could all be reduced to several more basic elements, and before long the modern version of the periodic table began to take shape. Finally, in 1869, Dmitri Mendeleev brought these developments to a head when he produced a periodic table in which the known chemical elements were arranged in terms of their specific densities and chemical properties. It immediately became clear, however, that the table contained several gaps; and accordingly, Mendeleev predicted the existence of several undiscovered elements, their specific densities, and their chemical properties. Other anomalies were also evident in the table but were cleared up when the accepted specific densities for some of the elements were found to be in error. When these errors were corrected, the consistency of the table was considerably improved.

Under the impetus given to chemical and atomic research by the periodic table, the theory of the atom also began to take shape. In 1913 Ernest Rutherford provided the key in his suggestion that the atom is composed of a nucleus of protons and neutrons surrounded by orbiting electrons. This new theory of the atom, however, implied that the elements consisted of several isotopes; and when this suggestion was acted upon and the elements refined into their isotopes, the few remaining discrepancies in the periodic table were resolved. It became perfectly regular. Thus, when a valid typology of the elements was finally hit upon by Mendeleev, it stimulated theoretical speculation about the fundamental nature of the elements, which in turn helped considerably to clarify the precise nature of the original typology.

Once the typologies that are relevant to delinquency have been perfected in this fashion, the final step in arriving at a comprehensive explanation of the problem is their articulation, by means of field theory, to give a synthetic typology of delinquency. Field theory is indispensable at this point because it allows the theorist to coordinate the implications of two or more basically distinct force-systems without also assuming that they can be reduced to a single system. It provides the framework in its concepts of the life-space and the situation that allows one to think about the impact of psychological forces upon the social system, and social forces upon the personality, without also assuming that the social system is epiphenomenal to the personality or that the personality is simply a reflection of the social system. Without this kind of conceptual bridge, the theory of social action would be an idle exercise. Using field theory intelligently, however, it is possible to construct a synthetic typology of every aspect of social action including delinquency.

Curiously enough, these suggestions regarding the development of a synthetic typology of social action run somewhat counter to the admonitions of Lewin regarding the explanation of behavior.[21] Lewin maintained that the Aristotelian method of developing concepts based upon the similarities of a class— the classificatory method—was impractical because it leads to concepts that are less and less relevant to the actual individuals being studied. The concept, Homo sapiens, for example, provides little information regarding the wide range of characteristics that members of this class exhibit and, consequently, little basis for predicting their behavior.

A better method, according to Lewin, is one in which concepts are developed by weaving several causal factors together into an explanation so that the significant characteristics of each individual are fully accounted for. The constructive method, as Lewin called it, was the preferred method of developing a science of behavior because it did not result in an increasing logical distance between the conceptual models and the individuals that the models were supposed to explain. Indeed, quite the reverse was the case, for as more causal factors were integrated into the model, more facets of the individual became explainable.

The classificatory method, according to Lewin, leads only to phenotypes that summarize the superficial similarities of a class, but the constructive method leads to the definition of genotypes that group together individuals with essential similarities. Clearly, Lewin's constructive method is the method suggested above for the development of a synthetic typology.

It must be pointed out, however, that the definition of an empirical typology, which is the first step in the construction of an ideal typology, is probably best accomplished by means of the same classificatory method for which Lewin had so little use. In order to formulate a heuristic vocabulary for the analysis of behavior it is necessary to identify, first, the phenotypes that exist in the population. Once the conceptual dimensions of the phenotypes have been carefully identified, hypothetical constructs can be suggested to explain their characteristics and eventually genotypic explanations developed. The whole edifice of science, therefore, rests in the last analysis upon the untutored observation of novices who in the course of their haphazard experimentation have developed a classificatory method to give order to their observations. To spurn them and their methods would be to spurn the very foundation of scientific insight and explanation.

NOTES

[1] Jack P. Gibbs, "Needed: Analytical Typologies in Criminology," *Southwestern Social Science Quarterly*, Vol. 40, No. 3 (March, 1960), pp. 321–29.

[2] Don C. Gibbons and D. L. Garrity, "Some Suggestions for the Development of Etiological and Treatment Theory in Criminology," *Social Forces*, Vol. 38, No. 1 (October, 1959), pp. 51–57.

[3] Julian Roebuck, "A Criticism of Gibbon's and Garrity's Criminal Typology," *Journal of Criminal Law, Criminology, and Police Science*, Vol. 54, No. 4 (December, 1963), pp. 476–78.

[4] J. C. McKinney and A. C. Kerckhoff, "Toward a Codification of Typological Procedure," *Sociological Inquiry*, Vol. XXXII, No. 1 (Winter, 1962), pp. 128–35.

[5] Burkart Holzner and John K. Rhoads, "The Logic of Type Construction," *Archiv für Rechts und Sozialphilosophie*, Vol. XLVII, No. 4 (November, 1961), pp. 541–52.

[6] Carl G. Hempel, "Symposium: Problems of Concept and Theory Formation in the Social Sciences," *Science, Language, and Human Rights*, Vol. 1 (Philadelphia: University of Pennsylvania Press, 1952), pp. 65–80.

[7] Marvin E. Wolfgang, "Cesare Lombroso," in Hermann Mannheim, ed., *Pioneers in Criminology* (Chicago: Quadrangle Books, 1960), pp. 182–90.

[8] *Ibid.*, p. 185.

9 Lester E. Hewitt and Richard L. Jenkins, *Fundamental Patterns of Maladjustment* (Springfield, Illinois: State Printer, 1947), pp. 25–74.

10 See Albert J. Reiss, Jr., "Social Correlates of Psychological Types of Delinquency," *American Sociological Review*, Vol. 17, No. 6 (December, 1952), pp. 710–18; R. Nevitt Sanford, "A Psychoanalytic Study of Three Criminal Types," *Journal of Criminal Psychopathology*, Vol. 5, No. 1 (July, 1943), pp. 57–68; Kate Friedlander, *The Psychoanalytic Approach to Juvenile Delinquency* (New York: International Universities Press, 1947), pp. 84–187; and Franz Alexander and Hugo Staub, *The Criminal, the Judge, and the Public,* 2d ed. (New York: Free Press, 1956), pp. 83–124.

11 The point here is that there are several different functions that typologies can fulfill in the analysis of behavior. They are all important, and no single kind of typology can serve them all adequately. Hence, there is no *single* set of criteria that describes the qualities that all typologies should exhibit, as the authors mentioned in the first paragraphs of this chapter seem to suggest.

12 See Alex Inkeles, "Personality and Social Structure," in Robert K. Merton, ed., *Sociology Today* (New York: Basic Books, 1959), pp. 272–75, for a recent statement of the need for psycho-sociological explanations of social systems and for social psychological explanations of individual behavior.

13 Sheldon and Eleanor Glueck seem to have tried something quite similar in their attempts to explain the delinquency of mesomorphic, ectomorphic, and endomorphic delinquents. See their work, *Physique and Delinquency* (New York: Harper & Row, 1956), pp. 219–41.

14 Kurt Lewin, *Field Theory in Social Science,* Dorwin Cartwright, ed. (New York: Harper, 1951), p. 45.

15 *Ibid.,* pp. 238–41.

16 I have already indicated in Chapter Two, pp. 28–37, how forces at different levels can interrelate, and the discussion is carried further in this chapter, pp. 67–69.

[17] See note 16, above.

[18] This discussion suggests, as Freud contended, that the unconscious plays a strategic role in the psychology of civilized man. The unconscious allows him to repress facets of himself that are particularly disgusting and disconcerting to those around him. It allows, in other words, those who would otherwise be thrown into deep conflict with civilization to find an honorable position in society, even though it involves a denial of an important side of their individuality. The unconscious allows the individual to surmount the basic discrepancies between his own nature and society; and, thus, enables a much larger proportion of mankind to participate in the forms of society than would otherwise be able.

[19] See Chapter One, pp. 7–8, for a discussion of the distinction between essential and proximate causes.

[20] Don C. Gibbons, "Offender Types and the Study of Causation," *California Youth Quarterly,* Vol. 15, No. 1 (Spring, 1962), p. 13.

[21] Lewin, *Field Theory,* pp. 60–61.

CHAPTER 4

A Social Typology of Delinquency

In the last chapter we saw that the scientific study of delinquency should ultimately yield a synthetic typology that will enable us to diagnose accurately and to treat effectively most forms of delinquent behavior. We also saw that a synthetic typology essentially represents a skillful blending of ideal typologies and that it can be only as valid, precise, and exhaustive as the ideal typologies from which it is derived. A necessary step, therefore, in the formulation of a synthetic typology of delinquency is the identification and preparation of the basic ideal typologies that are directly relevant to delinquent behavior. There are, of course, several theoretical viewpoints that might be used in developing a typology of delinquent behavior —e.g., the social, the legal, the psychological, and the physiological—but in this discussion I shall be concerned with only two: the social and the psychological.

A social typology is essential to the explanation of delinquency because it summarizes succinctly the characteristic ways in which social forces combine to channel the behavior of adolescents in a delinquent direction. Each one of us behaves in the context of social situations that explicitly endorse certain courses of action while at the same time prohibiting others. And, depending upon the condition of our life-spaces, we may either conform to the socially suggested

courses of action or we may behave less conventionally. But whatever path our behavior follows, there
can be little doubt that it is influenced profoundly by
the situation immediately at hand. Therefore, since a
social typology of delinquency attempts to identify the
social force-fields that are relevant to delinquency and
to describe how these fields give rise to situations
conducive to delinquency, it is basic to the explanation of delinquent behavior.

A social typology of behavior, however, will not in
general describe the behavior of anyone perfectly.
Since everyone is exposed to forces beyond those included in his social field, the pattern of behavior the
individual finally elects will not usually reflect in
clear outline the influence of *any single* system of
forces. The absence of clear resolution, however,
should not be regarded as an open invitation to
buttress our sociological explanations with nonsocial
factors before the social forces themselves have been
carefully identified. There is always a temptation to
explain that which is complex by that which is most
immediate, but in this case resorting prematurely to
nonsocial factors would only mask the influence of
social forces upon human behavior and distort their
significance. It is essential, therefore, that a social
typology be framed solely at the social level of analysis
and that it be defined solely in terms of sociological
theories.

Moreover, it must be concerned not only with those
forces that actively promote delinquent behavior but
also with those that inhibit and suppress it. The forces
that directly mold delinquent standards are, of course,
fundamental to the formulation of a social typology of
delinquent behavior. But we must also recognize that
the emergence of institutionalized delinquency de-

pends as much upon the forces resisting its appearance as it does upon those supporting its development. Hence, to arrive at a valid social typology we must identify not only those forces that give structure and definition to delinquent action, but also those forces that weaken and suppress it.

Finally, a social typology of delinquency must focus primarily upon those social forces that bear directly upon the individual, i.e., those forces that are immediately relevant to the delinquent's behavior. Theoretical viewpoints that deal primarily with systems of groups, for example, sociological functionalism or conflict theory, are of little immediate value in the derivation of a social typology. But those viewpoints that deal in the main with the reactions of individuals to the exigencies of structured interaction, e.g., sociological formalism, should be of considerable utility to the present analysis.[1] To be sure, functional theory and conflict theory may be of some value in identifying the social forces that shape the environment of delinquent groups, but it is sociological formalism that indicates how a group adjusts to these forces and how these adjustments affect its members.

There are, no doubt, a wide variety of social forces that are relevant to the forms of delinquency. Nevertheless, we shall only consider here three general types of forces: (1) those that arise in the social processes of a delinquent group; (2) those that arise in the class structure of the community; and (3) those arising in the family, school, and community to discourage delinquent behavior.

Each of these generic forces, of course, has its own characteristic impact upon adolescent behavior, but the specific criminogenic situations that adolescents confront can only be grasped when we have examined the confluence of these forces in a social field and identified their typical patterns of interaction. Let us turn, then, to an examination of the specific nature of each of these forces so that we may later in the chapter consider their patterns of interaction.

Associations and Delinquency

The emergence of gang delinquency in a neighborhood does not represent simply a coalescence of delinquents who would have behaved in much the same manner had the group not developed. It means, in effect, that the severity of the problem is considerably compounded. Delinquency need no longer depend solely upon those adolescents who spontaneously exhibit deep anti-social feelings to serve as its partisans. As an institutionalized pattern it can begin to recruit from among those youngsters who have no personal inclinations in a delinquent direction, since it can bring pressures to bear upon them that no individual delinquent could ever muster. But delinquency not only becomes more entrenched as it becomes institutionalized, it also changes its basic nature.

There are at least four ways in which the induction of an adolescent into a delinquent grouping changes his behavior. First, it relieves him to some extent from the necessity of reconciling his chronically anti-social conduct with the values and standards that the rest of the community upholds. Second, it tends to amplify the intensity of each member's delinquent behavior. Third, the delinquent group's illegal status in the community forces it to develop an unusual solidarity and *esprit de corps*, which in turn strengthens its discipline over the individual. And finally, the interaction of the delinquent group with other groups, both delinquent and nondelinquent, forces it to spe-

cialize in certain types of delinquencies to the exclusion of others, focusing, therefore, the activities of its
members to a considerable degree. Let us examine
each of these processes in detail.

Nullifying the Community

It was Redl and Wineman who first noted the
ingenious rationalizations that delinquents utilize
among themselves to justify their particular form of
deviant behavior. They regarded these techniques as
attempts on the part of the individual's ego to ward
off intolerable feelings of guilt, and in the course of
their observations they were able to identify twelve
distinct "strategies of tax evasion."[2] It remained,
however, for Sykes and Matza to point out that many
of these mechanisms of defense are basically an integral part of the delinquent culture and that their
principal function is to *prevent* the self-reproach that
many delinquents would otherwise experience as a
consequence of their misdeeds.[3]

These authors suggest—as did Redl and Wineman
before them—that since delinquents subscribe to the
values of their community in much the same way that
everyone else does, when they violate its mores they
also experience severe pangs of guilt. To prevent these
guilt feelings, delinquents as a class are obliged to
develop a set of cultural myths that in effect absolve
each delinquent of responsibility for his anti-social
behavior. The actual myths themselves are nearly
infinite in number, and anyone who has had any
experience with delinquents has heard many of them
repeated with dismaying regularity. Sykes and Matza,
however, were able to identify five basic types: the
denial of responsibility, the denial of injury, the
denial of the victim, the condemnation of the con-

demners, and the appeal to higher loyalties. These techniques of neutralization, as described by Sykes and Matza, are well established in the delinquent culture; and through their web of associations, they are proffered to all delinquents regardless of the nature of their personality or the manner in which they deal with guilt internally.

The fact of their delinquency, then, throws delinquents into direct conflict with the basic mores of their community and forces them as a class to develop and perpetuate a series of protective techniques that serve to immunize them from the censure—both external and internal—of the community. *Any* delinquent who associates with other delinquents cannot help being exposed to these cultural rationalizations and eventually using them to justify his deviancy. In effect, then, institutionalized delinquency intervenes between the individual delinquent and the larger community and with these myths nullifies some of its most effective methods of control.

The effectiveness of these techniques of neutralization undoubtedly depends to some extent upon the solidarity of the delinquent group: the more cohesive the group, the more effective the techniques in preventing its members from feeling guilty. But it is probably also true that the rationalizations themselves are readily exchanged by delinquents whenever it becomes apparent that they share a delinquent status. These culturally based techniques express a point of view that all delinquents can readily appreciate, and they are shared by most delinquents, even those who have only a fleeting association with other delinquents.

Group Structure: A Catalytic Agent

The emergence of a group structure among mildly delinquent youngsters also considerably shapes and focuses their delinquent tendencies. As delinquent associations crystallize in the form of cliques and gangs, a definite structure emerges in which one or a few boys assume formal leadership over the rest.[4] This added dimension in their relationships, however, results in an extraordinary transformation of their behavior. The leadership nucleus is usually drawn from among those boys whose delinquent identities are most firmly established and for whom delinquent exploits are a confirmed pattern.[5] For them the gang and its activities provide a convenient medium through which certain of their deepest feelings can be expressed openly and unambiguously. Although many of the leaders would probably have been delinquent without the gang, the presence of the gang as a vehicle for their anti-social sentiments serves to aggravate their delinquent tendencies appreciably. The mild approval or respect of the other members is frequently enough to inspire the leaders to even more dangerous and serious kinds of delinquencies than would have been committed had they been acting alone.[6]

Even though the rank and file in the gang are less firmly committed to a delinquent pattern of behavior, their membership in the gang also serves to intensify their delinquent behavior in much the same fashion. The discipline of the gang obliges them to participate in most of its activities, and since the gang's leadership by its very nature is more daring, imaginative, and anti-social than the rest, the rank and file are often persuaded to undertake many delinquent actions they would never dream of performing if left to themselves. Hence, the structuring of a delinquent group in terms of authority brings powerful social forces to bear upon its members, with the over-all result that the delinquent behavior of all concerned is considerably amplified.

The social forces that are released upon the members in this fashion, however, are not equally available to all types of social groups. Only those groups that have developed a shared code of values and a regular pattern of association can support a structuring of their relationships in terms of authority. Under these conditions, however, the office of the leader with all its prerogatives and responsibilities clearly emerges in the minds of the members, and they readily identify who among them is best-fitted to act in this capacity. For these reasons, then, casual associations among delinquents are not a sufficient basis for a clear authority structure; and although cliques are sufficiently cohesive to support one, when it does emerge, the added structure also quickly transforms them into gangs.[7] Hence, only gangs are likely to exhibit a clearly defined authority structure and its catalytic effects upon delinquent behavior.

The Implications of Illegitimacy

An emergent gang, moreover, is promptly confronted by the implications of its emergence. It is typically regarded in the community with fear and abhorrence, and the individual members are made painfully aware that their membership in the gang is regarded by their relatives, neighbors, and teachers as a serious blot upon their characters. Thus, the emergence of a delinquent gang tends to range against it most groups that are closely identified with the moral foundations of the community and to call into very serious question the bases of its legitimacy.

In response to these pressures most delinquent groups are forced to develop arguments emphasizing two basic themes: the gang and its members are superior in most respects to its critics; and the values of its detractors are ridiculous and of little authority among those who really count.[8] Thus, the gang asserts, on the one hand, that its activities are eminently virtuous and, on the other, that in judging the gang as illegitimate its critics reveal their own moral depravity.

These assertions, however, must not be confused with the techniques of neutralization discussed above. They are not framed primarily to protect the members from the criticism and condemnation of the community. Rather, the gang's protestations about its moral validity are calculated mainly to preserve its sovereignty over its members. They represent an attempt to persuade the members collectively that their membership in the gang is highly admirable and worthwhile.

Most gangs, then, evolve not only arguments defending their own moral worth, but also devastating critiques of just those groups that are most vigorous in their condemnation. If the gang can convince its members that its principal detractors are themselves on indefensible moral grounds, their condemnations are weakened considerably. But whether its arguments are in defense of the group's own legitimacy or in criticism of other groups, the question of its legitimacy remains a very tender issue. Most delinquent gangs, therefore, go to great lengths to encourage a system of values among their members that is the obverse of that in the larger community.

According to several observers, the gang's principal antagonist is the middle class.[9] Since working-class youngsters are routinely thrown into conflict with middle-class teachers in the public schools, the more difficult youngsters often come to regard the middle class as their mortal enemies and to visit their aggressions generally upon the members of this class. There is, of course, considerable evidence to support this view. The depredations of working-class delinquents are frequently directed against middle-class institutions like the high schools and the churches, and the garb of urban delinquents could scarcely be more irritating and annoying to the sensibilities of proper middle-class individuals. In the street, the delinquents' grotesque costumes almost invariably strike a mixture of fear and contempt in the hearts of good middle-class citizens.

In some communities this antagonism between working-class delinquents and middle-class adolescents has progressed to the point where it assumes the characteristics of open warfare. The struggle has colloquially been termed a contest between the long hairs—the delinquents—and the short hairs—the college-bound, middle-class youngsters; and it consists, in the main, of periodic forays by delinquents against middle-class adolescents at drive-ins, football games, parties, and dances, i.e., wherever middle-class adolescents celebrate their cultural rituals. The middle class, however, is not the only nor perhaps even the major antagonist of these working-class gangs. Thrasher suggests, for example, that gangs are *most* generally aggressive toward the police and other gangs in the community.[10]

But whether its antagonism is directed against a whole social class or a specific rival group, the gang's morally shaky position generally requires it to repudiate the rival group's values and to adopt their polar opposites.

If the middle class sanctifies private property and esteems a "nice" appearance, the gang must destroy middle-class property and assume a bizarre, threatening appearance. If rival gang members pride themselves on their fighting ability, the gang must challenge and, if possible, destroy the basis of their pride. *Because the delinquent gang is delinquent, it cannot tolerate other groups that directly challenge its own legitimacy.* The values of the gang, therefore, must bolster its solidarity by undermining the legitimacy of its principal antagonists, whatever their orientation. In certain respects, then, the culture of the gang represents a reaction against the dominant values and groups in the community.

Community Organization and Delinquency

According to Cloward and Ohlin, a fourth factor that plays an important part in shaping the values of the delinquent gang is the organization of its community.[11] The orientation of the gang, i.e., whether it is a fighting gang or a criminal gang, depends basically upon the manner in which several different kinds of groups interrelate in the community. The criminal gang, for example, tends to develop primarily in those communities where conventional, criminal, and adolescent groups are all integrated to form a highly solidary community.[12] The close integration of criminal and conventional elements in the community allows the criminal stratum to stabilize and perfect its organization, while at the same time the more conventional stratum is able to impose many subtle controls over criminal operations. It is a very useful arrangement for both factions and serves to reinforce their mutual investment in the community.

The more successful criminals in such communities often enjoy many of the privileges and appurtenances of upper-class status, and, accordingly, they often serve as convenient models for ambitious youngsters in the community to follow. Moreover, the influence that established criminals wield over adolescents in this fashion forms the basis for a "feeder" system in which the successful adults in crime train the teenagers in the community in the arts and crafts of their particular form of criminality.

In this fashion, then, the close tie-ins that organized crime enjoys both with the adolescents and with conventional groups enable it to play a decisive role in shaping delinquent gangs in the community. It encourages the gang to specialize in offenses that are disciplined and utilitarian—offenses that demonstrate the adolescent's criminal potential—while at the same time it discourages malicious, wantonly destructive crimes that testify essentially to the adolescent's irresponsibility and lack of control.

The community organization most closely associated with the fighting gang differs in several respects from the one we have just considered.[13] In the first place, the community is considerably more disorganized at all levels. Although conventional groups are definitely opposed to crime, the web of controls in the community has largely collapsed, and their efforts at controlling criminal behavior are basically ineffectual. In spite of their ineffectiveness, however, much of the crime is unsophisticated, small-scale, and fumbling, whereas the efforts of conventional individuals along more legitimate lines of endeavor are scarcely more successful. Thus, the absence of real career opportunities of either a conventional or criminal sort arouses among the adolescents considerable frustration; and with the lack of effective social controls in the community, their frustration is most typically expressed in the form of violent attacks upon other adolescent groups in the community.

Violence is an especially attractive mode of expression for two reasons. It helps vent some of the status-frustration so common among the adolescents in these communities, and it helps the youngsters prove themselves worthy in the eyes of their associates. No matter how damning their other characteristics and weaknesses may be, their detractors have no choice but to defer to the threat of violence, for to do otherwise is to invite their own destruction. Viciousness and strength, then, in the disorganized community play much the same role that intelligence and industriousness play in the organized community. They serve as criteria whereby the individual's status in the community is determined.

Cloward and Ohlin also describe a third type of gang—the retreatist gang—in which the principal delinquent activity is the use of narcotics.[14] Such gangs are not directly shaped by the organization of their community, since they include only those adolescents who for one reason or another are unable to enter other types of delinquent gangs or more legitimate lines of activity that lead eventually to success in the conventional world. The retreatist gang, then, is the last stop for those adolescents who are denied admission to all other forms of association. It will occur in organized as well as disorganized communities, that is, wherever there are enough interested individuals to form a group. Its membership, however, will probably include a disproportionate number of seriously disor-

ganized individuals; and for this reason it is likely to be most common where large numbers of such adolescents exist, i.e., in disorganized communities.

In this manner, then, Cloward and Ohlin explain the development of adolescent gangs pursuing distinctly different forms of delinquency. It should be noted, however, that their analysis of the forces behind these gangs is not exclusively confined to social factors. Although the objectives of the criminal gang depend primarily upon the aims of the criminal faction in the community, both the fighting and the retreatist gangs are defined much more in terms of the individualistic reactions of their members to the structure of their communities.

For the criminal gang the community is both the author of its lines and the director of its actions. For the fighting and retreatist gangs, however, social forces no longer have a major voice in composing the lines or in directing the action. Instead, the values of *these* two gangs are shaped mainly by the spontaneous reactions of individuals to their disorganized situations. To be sure, socially based frustration and hopelessness are the stimuli behind the values of these gangs; but to explain the precise nature of their cultural patterns, it is necessary to identify not only the sources of frustration and hopelessness in the community but also the *psychological* forces behind their members' aggressive and withdrawal reactions.

But in terms of sociological theory, there is no reason to expect any *particular* type of reaction from the members of fighting and retreatist gangs. It is inappropriate, therefore, to consider these two types of gangs as members of a social typology of delinquent gangs. Although there are delinquent gangs whose behavioral patterns do not essentially reflect the influ-

ence of *social* forces, (and according to Cloward and
Ohlin fighting and retreatist gangs clearly fall in this
category) a social typology of gangs cannot reasonably
include them as members.

The Class Structure and Delinquency

In our attempt to derive a social typology of delinquent behavior, we have shown how a wide variety of
social forces mold delinquent behavior; but we have
not yet considered perhaps the most significant of
all—social class. It is common knowledge, however,
that an individual's attitude and beliefs, his values
and aspirations, and, indeed, his whole way of life are
determined to a very considerable extent by his class
position.

Walter Miller was one of the first to examine this
proposition as it relates specifically to the delinquent,
and it was his contention that members of the "lower
class"—whether adolescent or adult—subscribe to a
set of focal concerns that inevitably throw them into
conflict with the legal code in their community.[15]
Thus, for example, the attractiveness of activities that
"get one into trouble" and in some cases the prestige
that getting into trouble itself confers invite the lower-
class person to consider violating the laws of his
community. Second, the preoccupation of the lower-
class male with toughness and masculinity tends to
encourage him to use violent forms of expression,
which may occasionally lead to felonious assault and,
again, serious difficulty with the law. Third, the
esteem that shrewdness and exploitative "conman-
ship" are accorded in the lower class inclines the
average member to improve his own situation at the
expense of someone else and often results, inciden-

tally, in illegal behavior. Fourth, the addiction of the lower-class person to thrills and excitement leads him to court danger; and, as a result, he frequently finds himself violating the established norms of his community. And finally, the vigilance of the typical lower-class person that he not be pushed around—together with his deep desire to be comprehensively, if not lovingly, cared for by the community—inclines him to resist lawful authority, while at the same time accepting passively whatever fate may bring. Thus, according to Miller, by conforming systematically to a lower-class style of life, the average member of that class runs a high risk of violating the basic laws of his society, which unfortunately for him are defined in terms of a different set of focal concerns.

Other authors have argued in a similar vein that the prevailing values and practices of particular groups in society incline their members toward distinctive types of illegal activities.[16] But no one thus far has undertaken a systematic examination of the value systems of the several social classes making up American society to identify whether they also provide subtle encouragement for certain types of delinquent activity.

Let us attempt to remedy this deficiency by examining carefully the value systems of the classes in a typical American community to determine how they stimulate a characteristic pattern of delinquent activity among adolescent members of each class.

Without becoming embroiled in the controversy that has surrounded the definition and measurement of social class in recent years, I shall assume, along with W. Lloyd Warner, that there are three major social classes in most urban communities—an upper, a middle, and a lower class—and that in many communities these are further divided into upper and lower subclasses.[17]

It must be recognized, of course, that the Warner schema leaves something to be desired as a description of the class structure of American cities. First, not every city can support a full complement of six classes, and, second, the reputational method as developed by Warner is certainly inapplicable where the members of a class are largely anonymous even to one another. Nevertheless, Warner's critics have not yet provided a schema that does describe *all* cities, and the deficiencies of the reputational method do not necessarily destroy the validity of the six-layered class structure envisioned by Warner. Thus, in my judgment, the most adequate basis for a discussion of American class structure is that provided by Warner; and, accordingly, I am assuming that in general there are six separate and distinct social strata and that the adolescent members of these several classes subscribe to distinctive cultural patterns that set them unmistakably apart from one another.

Because the upper upper-class has been the subject of considerable interest both in popular and scientific literature, it is most convenient to begin our examination with this class.

The Upper Upper-Class and Delinquency

The key to the upper upper-class and its cultural patterns is basically found in the functions it performs in the community and the society.[18] Essentially, the functions of the upper upper-class are twofold: it provides a cadre of seasoned and responsible leaders to guide the community in its cultural, economic, and political affairs; and this class ensures the preservation of the "best" traditions of the community by incorporating them into the normative patterns of family groups and intensively socializing the youth in them. Much that is noteworthy and significant for human culture is embodied in the traditions of upper upper-class families or kinship groups and thereby preserved for the community and society as a whole.

Their pre-eminence, however, does not sit lightly. Because they are born to their position, they must justify their aristocratic pretensions in terms of standards that are not based entirely or even primarily upon achievement and performance. They must, in short, discredit all nonmembers who might qualify for leadership positions in terms of their achievements but who do not qualify for aristocratic status.[19]

The distinctive upper upper-class style that has evolved in many American communities has been carefully chronicled by several observers. In Philadelphia, for example, they are described as casual and relaxed, oriented more to pleasure and comfort than to achievement or work, and dedicated to preserving their distinctive position and way of life. Their motto is "moderation in all things," and their ideal is "Good Form."[20] In Elmtown the upper upper-class feels that its position is based upon a superior genetic endowment, and it stresses the importance of breeding—the ability to know and instinctively to do the right thing in most situations—as an index of quality and upper upper-class membership. How a person performs his occupation is of less importance than how he spends his leisure time—and with whom. And there is little regard for conventional morality, although there is little or no criminality.[21]

The typical upper upper-class person occupies his position because of his breeding, which in turn can be

readily recognized in his appearance, in his posses-
sions, in his talents, and in his skill in dealing with
others. The standards of good taste are well known in
the upper upper-class, and there is considerable pressure on all sides to observe these standards at least to a
minimal degree. Minor lapses, however, if not chronic
or uncontrollable, merely testify to the exquisite individualism of the person, not to his lack of refinement.

The upper upper-class person also typically repudi-
ates the standards of the other classes. The aggressive
industriousness of the lower upper- and upper middle-
classes, the sterile asceticism of the lower middle-class,
and the unbridled impulsiveness of the lower classes
are all denied as unworthy. The mores of the larger
community, however, are founded upon some of these
same values that the upper upper-class person so
quickly dismisses. And since he does not feel bound by
the same moral and legal codes that govern the rest of
the community, he may at times do things that scan-
dalize those in the community who do not share his
values and position.[22]

Among upper upper-class adolescents these values
and ideals should give rise to a distinctive pattern of
anti-social behavior. The emphasis upon good form
and moderation, for example, probably precludes
most kinds of violence against the person. The average
adolescent in this class regards such uncontrolled outbursts as more typical of the lower classes and, therefore, completely out of the question for himself.

The emphasis upon style and form in the upper
upper-class, however, probably *does* mean that the
typical adolescent cultivates a manner that is distinctive and personalistic but that at the same time clearly
indicates a superior breeding. Many upper upper-class
youngsters in establishing a personalistic manner, may

be tempted to indulge in certain excesses that are not
as vicious as they are indicative of a superb sense of
style. The debutante party in Southampton, which
resulted in the virtual demolition of a beach house, is
a case in point.[23] The animating spirit in the destruction was not so much maliciousness as a straining for
the extraordinary. The youngsters involved were not
venting a pent-up rage against society—far from it,
they were hoping to establish their own uniqueness,
their own quality in a distinctive and unusual way.

The conviction, then, among the upper upper-class
that quality and breeding are readily identified in the
style of the individual is likely to lead the members of
this class generally and the adolescents in particular to
place this value above more conventional ones and to
indulge in offenses that establish the individual as a
person with style. These offenses are not likely to
involve assaults upon the person, but they *are* likely to
take the form of mischief—e.g., the destruction of
property as in the Southampton debutante party—
and the wrongful appropriation of property—e.g., the
stealing of an auto and other articles on a lark.

The lack of sympathy in the upper upper-class for
many aspects of conventional middle-class morality
also contributes to the distinctive character of delinquency found in this class. For example, there are few
prohibitions against the use of alcohol in most upper
upper-class families, and accordingly, many upper
upper-class adolescents see nothing wrong in using
alcohol at least in moderation.[24] But in states where
the purchase or use of alcohol by adolescents is controlled by law, upper upper-class youngsters are very
likely to be delinquent with some frequency. And, in
similar fashion, the absence of powerful prohibitions
against sexual indulgence in the upper upper-class,

together with the intense interest that all adolescents have in such matters, undoubtedly results in considerable sexual experimentation among male upper upper-class teenagers. Their sexual activities, however, are probably more expressive than exploitative, and they are very unlikely to involve the outright coercion of the partner. We might expect to find, therefore, considerable amount of illicit sexual intercourse and other kinds of sexual indulgence that are technically illegal but very little actual rape.

Essentially, then, the normative patterns of the upper upper-class seem to encourage two types of delinquent activity among its more adventuresome youths. First, there should be considerable emphasis upon offenses involving the misappropriation or the reckless destruction of property. Second, there should also be an appreciable number of offenses of an indulgent character, i.e., sexual delinquencies and the illegal use and purchase of alcoholic beverages. The restraint of upper upper-class cultural patterns, however, seems to forbid any tendency toward violent, unprovoked offenses against the person; and their ample standard of living seems to preclude chronic theft, robbery, or burglary as a frequent pattern.

The Lower Upper- and Upper Middle-Classes

The lower upper-class differs quite sharply from the upper upper-class in both function and life style.[25] The function of the lower upper-class is not to preserve the best traditions of the community and society —quite the opposite. It is to indicate those customs, traditions, and beliefs that are outmoded and to replace them with innovations that are better suited to the needs of the modern age. Members of the lower upper-class are rarely radicals in that they do not often favor a dramatic break with the past, but they frequently are the authors of significant innovations in the cultural, economic, and political structures of their communities. If the function of the upper upper-class is essentially conservative, then that of the lower upper-class is basically progressive. Its contribution to the community rests more in its ability to improve and perfect traditions than to preserve and protect them.[26]

Because the members of this class have achieved an exalted position in the community largely through their own industry and ability, they generally feel somewhat less defensive or self-conscious about their status than their counterparts in the upper upper-class. Moreover, since their accomplishments are generally applauded by the community, they are not as likely to disdain the value-systems of the other classes. They may have certain reservations about the competency of individual members of the middle-classes, but they do not repudiate their values. Their sympathy for and, in many cases, roots in the middle-class tends to arouse in them a sincere attachment to conventional values, which in turn often prompts them to throw themselves into church, political, and social affairs in the community with great energy and enthusiasm. Moreover, their spirited endorsement of conventional values and forms, together with their extraordinary achievements, sometimes results in their apotheosis by the community, their individual careers coming to summarize for the community all that is admired and morally worthwhile. Thus, the members of the lower upper-class are generally quite visible to the rest of the community; they tend to endorse steadfastly the conventional morality of their community, and as a consequence of their unusual achievements, they are lionized and adored in every way by their community.[27]

In line with their role in the community, the lower upper-class is somewhat less elitist and somewhat more individualistic than the upper upper-class. Since they tend to judge others in terms of their ability and personal accomplishments, the highest qualities for them are alertness, intelligence and perseverance. Style and manner are not unimportant, but they are less important than productivity and results. Because achievement is of such surpassing importance, the members of this class are quite competitive in most facets of their behavior. They feel themselves under great pressure to excel; hence, their extraordinary vitality and enthusiasm in everything they undertake.

The adolescents in this class are confronted with the same pressures to prove themselves through performance, and consequently they, too, must compete and ultimately prevail in those activities that are meaningful in the community. But along with this emphasis upon achievement we also encounter among the males of this class a strong concern for masculinity. Although their image of masculinity is a far cry from that of the lower classes, the lower upper-class adolescent has a picture of the ideal male that obliges him to accept the challenge of all reasonable competitors, to compete according to the rules, and to triumph by virtue of his greater skill, endurance, and acuity. Physical strength is regarded as an asset in these encounters, but it is not the *sine qua non* of masculine virtue. The essential purpose of competition is to allow one to prove his *own* mettle, not to destroy his competitors. Hence, physical strength is valuable only as it complements and enhances one's own competitive ability and not as a weapon against others.

The adolescents of the lower upper-class are confronted, then, with a web of expectations that is centered largely upon the need to prove oneself by extraordinary achievement. Unlike upper upper-class youngsters, however, who must fit their personalities into a cultural pattern that abjures excess in any form, these youngsters must be ready to go all out in the pursuit of excellence.

Although competition among the males has been institutionalized along several different lines, for the gentler sex the institutionalized channels of competition are less well defined, and the criteria of success and failure are somewhat more ambiguous. Among lower upper-class girls, therefore, competition tends to follow a more personalistic path.

The types of adolescent behavior that are implied by the cultural patterns we have just outlined are not difficult to define. In view of the significance of competition for the lower upper-class adolescent, determining both the level of his ability and the quality of his masculinity, the typical male in this class is exposed to great pressure to enter into vigorous, disciplined competition.

One of the most suitable outlets in this connection is certainly high school athletics—basketball and especially football serving admirably. But because the varsity teams are small in comparison with the numbers seeking positions, only a small minority of the lower upper-class males can distinguish themselves in this fashion. Competition for grades is not as adequate for establishing one's worth—although lower upper-class youngsters compete vigorously here too—since it tests only intellectual ability, not endurance or physical agility. Most adolescents in this class, therefore, are afforded little opportunity to establish themselves as worthy individuals through institutionalized forms of competition. They must of necessity find other, less standardized media in which to establish their masculine identities and personal abilities.

Certainly, one of the most convenient media for the adolescents of this class is the adolescent society, since it is generally accessible to those youngsters who attend the public schools in their communities. According to Coleman, the adolescent society achieves its fullest development in those schools that are involved in intercommunity athletic competition, that are coed, and that serve a well-defined and solidary community.[28] Thus, upper upper-class children largely escape its influence, because for the most part they are educated in private preparatory schools that are not coeducational and that do not represent any tangible community in contests with other schools. The same is also true, of course, of those lower upper-class children who attend private schools. But those who attend the public high schools are likely to play a central role in the adolescent society, since they, together with their counterparts in the upper middle-class, often serve as a nucleus for the teenagers as a group.[29]

Lower-middle and lower-class adolescents are admitted into the inner circle of the adolescent society only if they happen to excel at certain qualities highly esteemed by other adolescents. Most generally, however, they are seriously handicapped by their parents' lack of resources and their own lack of sophistication. The adolescent society, therefore, is largely a creation of lower upper- and upper middle-class adolescents with lower middle- and lower-class youngsters remaining for the most part on the margins of the prestigeful teenage cliques and clubs.

The values of the adolescent society, i.e., the adolescent culture, represent essentially the reaction of the adolescents as a group to social pressures emanating from the community as a whole. Although the values of the adolescents do not closely parallel those of the dominant adult groups in the community, they are pervasively influenced by these same groups. James Coleman's masterful study of the adolescent society suggests that athletics is important in establishing the adolescent's rank among his friends because the community as a whole demonstrates a consuming interest in the achievements of its high school athletic teams.

Since the high school represents the community in competition with other communities, its victory or defeat in athletic contests is a very tangible, if somewhat superficial, measure of the quality of the community in comparison with its nearest rivals. The symbolic significance of these high school games virtually forces those who identify with the community to involve themselves intimately with the teams and their fortunes. Their interest, of course, extends to the individual athletes themselves and, in turn, forms the basis for their popularity among their peers. Thus, the strategic role of high school athletics in the community establishes athletic ability as one of the most basic measures of individual worth among male adolescents.

The central position of athletes in the community, in turn, determines the criteria by which the girls might also distinguish themselves. Obviously, they cannot excel at athletics, but they can share some of the athlete's fame by aligning themselves with one of the star players. The handiest basis for such an alignment is, of course, sexual attraction. Thus, girls in the adolescent society are judged in terms of their ability to create a pleasing appearance that arouses in many subtle ways the sexual interests of the masculine and successful athlete.

According to Coleman, another element in the prestige of both boys and girls is their membership in one of the "leading crowds." But the standards by which members are selected for these cliques are basically the same as those defining an individual's rank. Hence, membership in these groups is more a confirmation of prestige than a determinant of prestige among adolescents. It simply certifies what everyone already knows, since an individual's achievement along lines that are appropriate to his sex must precede his becoming a member of one of the prestigeful cliques. Essentially, then, the adolescent society and its structure are founded upon two sex-linked qualities: athletic ability among the boys and personal attractiveness among the girls.[30]

The automobile also plays a strategic role in the adolescent society, although its importance is based upon the fact that it is a highly useful facility and not a basic value.[31] It symbolizes the socio-economic status of the adolescent's parents and, therefore, is useful in establishing the point at which he enters the adolescent society. It also serves as an especially convenient site for carrying on relationships with the opposite sex, and, finally, it is used by some youngsters as another means of demonstrating their competitive abilities through races and other kinds of driving tests. Thus, because the auto is instrumental in realizing several basic values in the adolescent society, it has itself become virtually indispensable to most adolescents. Its significance, however, should not be misinterpreted. It is not a value in its own right, it is simply a highly symbolic and adaptive tool.

The vigorous emergence of the adolescent society among lower upper- and upper middle-class youngsters carries many important implications for the nature of their delinquent behavior. In the first place, it forces the displacement of their parents and teachers as a shaping influence in favor of their peers and to some extent their coaches. The adolescents are busy playing an intensely exciting game that only they can fully appreciate; consequently, they tend to seek guidance and enlightenment not from the adults who are not involved in their games, but from their peers who are. In essence, this means that the members of the adolescent society will be relatively free psychologically to pursue any patterns of behavior that are prescribed and endorsed by their peers, whereas the ability of their parents and teachers to moderate or alter their behavior is considerably reduced.

Second, the importance attached to the development of a mildly erotic feminine manner among the girls stimulates passions that are already quite powerful among most male adolescents. Not only does the adolescent spontaneously feel a strong desire to engage the opposite sex, but he is actively encouraged to do so by his male friends in the adolescent society—and his desires are kept perpetually alive by the wiles and charms of his feminine classmates. The average member of the adolescent society is, thus, under well-nigh irresistible pressure to indulge his sexual appetites in some fashion whenever he can.

Finally, the strategic role of athletics and athletic ability among adolescents tends to inspire in the males an image of masculinity that centers upon strength, agility, and physical endurance. The ability to control and to organize one's behavior is not so important as the ability to react spontaneously and effectively.

Thus, the male is encouraged to be extroverted, and he is admired when his on-the-spot reactions display a certain finesse. The colorless, overcontrolled adolescent is shunned and ridiculed by everyone—even when he is the top student in his class.

Now, the emancipation of adolescents from significant control by adults, the intensification of their sexual desires, and the creation of a masculine image that encourages a dextrous impulsivity will not in themselves result in a significant amount of delinquent behavior. But when lower upper-class adolescents who are also under pressure to demonstrate their ability through competition come under the influence of the adolescent society and its values, it is easy to identify several delinquent patterns that are likely to appear with some frequency.

First, it is likely that many lower upper-class youngsters are going to express their competitive urges, indulge their sexual appetites, and enhance their prestige in the adolescent society all at the same time by throwing themselves wholeheartedly into the quest for sexual experience. Since there is a strong competitive aspect to their sexual activities, in which self-esteem is measured by experience, we can expect that the search for sexual partners will take an aggressive, almost frenetic quality. Thus, the lower upper-class male who is also a central figure in the cliques of his age-group is likely to regard sexual experience as the *summum bonum,* and he is likely to undertake a systematic and persistent campaign to broaden his knowledge and skill in this area.[32] Undoubtedly, in the course of his search, he will commit statutory rape—since a few of his feminine classmates are almost certain to become his sexual partners. And if he encounters an unwillingness on the part of some of them, it is entirely possible that he may insist to the point that he actually commits forcible rape. Moreover, sexual parties of various kinds are probably not uncommon among the adolescents of this class, although they probably do not involve lower upper-class girls as consistently as lower upper-class boys.

All in all, then, the lower upper-class youngster in the adolescent society is likely to give sexual experience the highest priority in his scheme of values and to pursue it aggressively. In contrast to upper upper-class youngsters, his orientation toward his feminine peers is definitely exploitative. Although he may also appreciate their other qualities, it is clear that their sexual capacities are of supreme importance.

The blossoming of the adolescent society among lower upper-class adolescents probably means, further, that violent, disorderly kinds of behavior in which considerable property is destroyed and individuals are more or less seriously injured will be rather common. The image of the male in the adolescent society as physically agile and resourceful, together with the lower upper-class emphasis upon proving one's worth through competition, will encourage certain males in this class to assume an openly belligerent, competitive attitude toward adolescents in rival communities or groups. Those lower upper-class males, for example, who have not been successful in high school athletics and who still feel pressed to demonstrate their manly qualities may resort to less organized kinds of competition, e.g., rumbles with the students from other high schools and vacation area riots. Finally, in view of the importance of automobiles to adolescents, these same kinds of aggressive values and ideals will undoubtedly be expressed in their driving style and result in serious violations of the traffic code in their community.

Much the same delinquent pattern is probably also typical of upper middle-class youngsters. Although the life style of the upper-middle class has not been studied with the same thoroughness as those of the two upper classes—Hollingshead ignores it entirely, and Warner provides only a brief sketch[33]—the major difference between the lower upper-class and this class seems to be mainly one of degree. For example, the pressure upon the individual to perform at a rarified level of success is somewhat less. Since really extraordinary achievement is considerably less frequent here than in the lower upper-class, the competitive aggressiveness of the upper middle-class probably does not approach that found in the lower upper-class. But upper middle-class individuals still evaluate one another in terms of their achievements, and the adolescents in this class are still absorbed in the activities of the adolescent society. The upper middle-class adolescent is thus governed by much the same cultural pattern that prevails in the lower upper-class, and, consequently, he is likely to exhibit much the same delinquent pattern. His sexual delinquencies are probably somewhat less aggressive and exploitative, and he is probably slightly less likely to carry his competitive impulses to violent extremes, but he conforms to the same general delinquent pattern typical of youngsters in the lower upper-class.

The Lower Middle-Class

The lower middle-class differs quite sharply from the upper middle- and lower upper-classes in both function and life style. It is up to the lower middle-class to perform the tiresome, routine duties that result from decisions made at higher levels in the community.[34] As a class, their economic services are indispensable, but as individuals, they are virtually indistinguishable from one another and, therefore, readily expendable. In reality, they rarely face unemployment, but the insecurity of their positions, together with their relatively slender incomes, is clearly reflected in their concern for thrift and their emphasis upon utility over style.

The marginality of their economic position is also largely responsible for their socially marginal position. They are accepted in the community, but because their economic contribution is anonymous, they have little basis for a claim to significant position.[35] They are respectable in the eyes of the higher classes, but they are lacking in the qualities that are necessary to social esteem; hence, they are not often accepted in the social activities of the upper classes. In general, then, the lower middle-class is only a sneeze away from economic and social bankruptcy, and this conditions its whole cultural pattern.

Since notable achievement is usually not the lot of its members, lower middle-class persons have no alternative but to overconform to the conventional values of the community in ritual fashion.[36] They cannot justify their position except by vigorously endorsing the same values and institutions that relegate them to a relatively inferior position in society. By confirming the position of the upper classes, however, they are able to win for themselves a tolerance, if not a genuine acceptance, at the middle level. And in their anxiety to establish themselves as decent citizens, they flock en masse to the conventionally respected churches, political organizations, and fellowship groups. The lower middle-class, therefore, composes the rank and file among the politically and socially significant organizations of the community. They carry little authority in these organizations, but they form the bulk of their membership.

The dominant concern in the lower middle-class, then, is their position in the community. Unlike the other classes they have no values properly their own that might inspire their endeavors to uncommon heights. Rather, they are forced to endorse an ethic, i.e., individualism, that leaves them socially insignificant. Hence, their value system provides not an inspiring ethos within which they might cultivate their skills and abilities, but a constricting admonition to avoid public rebuke.

It is difficult to see how such an ethos could lead to illegal activity for either adolescents or adults. If their position in the community depends primarily upon their ability to avoid serious censure, no lower middle-class person acting within the cultural pattern of his class will be inclined to violate the mores of his community. It would seem, therefore, that there is little in the life style of the lower middle-class to excite juvenile delinquency.

Moreover, as we have already noted, adolescents in this class are likely to be only marginally involved in the adolescent society. They certainly show the same fascination with the opposite sex that is typical of adolescents generally, but their marginal position in the adolescent society limits their chances to act upon their sexual fantasies, while at the same time it diminishes the peer-group pressures to seek out such opportunities. Similarly, they share with most adolescents a concern for their own identities, but their marginality with respect to the adolescent society blurs their concept of masculinity and weakens to some extent their desire to prove themselves through vigorous competition. Thus, the lower middle-class male is unlikely to

regard physical conflict as an acceptable way of establishing his masculinity. There is, therefore, very little
in this class or its values to encourage delinquent
behavior.

The Working Class

In the upper lower-class we find a much different
picture. The function of the upper lower-class is to
provide the manpower by which the community might
achieve its objectives, but, like the lower middle-class,
it is merely tolerated by the rest of the community.
The lower middle-class looks down upon the members
of this class, while they in turn feel embarrassed and
uncomfortable in the presence of individuals of higher
status.[37] Moreover, among themselves they often express feelings of resentment toward the higher classes,
maintaining that they are exploitative and insin-
cere.[38] Thus, the upper lower-class has very little
authority in the community, while at the same time it
is suspicious and resentful toward those who do.

Another facet of the upper lower-class cultural pattern is its conception of masculinity. Several authors
have noted that the male in this class is especially
sensitive to slights of any kind and that he is quick to
answer insults with verbal and, if necessary, physical
violence.[39] His picture of himself as a competent,
effective individual is not sufficiently stable to withstand severe criticism, hence his sensitivity to any
suggestion that he is not worthy and his desire to
squelch any such suggestion when it arises. The upper
lower-class individual does not seek out competition
in the same manner as the lower upper-class person;
rather, he prefers to avoid it, since it generally means
his defeat and/or embarrassment. But if anyone is so
foolhardy as to challenge him directly, he responds

like a wounded lion and attacks his tormentor with a vengeance. Repeated outbursts of this type are regarded in the higher classes as neurotic, but in the upper lower-class the mildest of insults quickly becomes an *affair d'honneur* requiring satisfaction. Thus, the concept of masculinity that is prevalent in the upper lower-class requires the male to meet *any* direct challenge with courage and to silence it with all the force and skill at his command.

Finally, the upper lower-class is unusually attracted to the extraordinary and exciting.[40] Since his usual round is rather dull, the upper lower-class person typically finds a certain satisfaction in occasionally breaking out of his humdrum existence in several different ways. Drinking bouts, sexual adventures, sports, gambling, and vital events among relatives and friends all serve to leaven an otherwise drab and uninteresting routine, and the typical upper lower-class person comes to cultivate and relish such distractions for this reason.

The adolescent in the upper lower-class is, of course, governed by these same values, with the result that his delinquent behavior unfolds in characteristic fashion. For example, the suspicion and resentment of his class toward the upper classes is sometimes expressed in a direct repudiation of authority figures representing the interests of these classes, e.g., the police and the school. But challenging the authority of these groups is in itself a delinquent act; hence, there is some encouragement in the upper lower-class for its adolescents to be ungovernable and disorderly with respect to the police and truant with respect to the school.

The conception of masculinity that is maintained in this class also encourages several distinctive delinquent patterns. First, Walter Miller has noted the

readiness with which upper lower-class youngsters resort to force and violence as a way of settling disputes,
and there can be little doubt that one source of these
assaultive tendencies is an image of the male as someone who quickly and effectively silences criticism.[41]
Hence, the upper lower-class adolescent is occasionally
prompted by his culturally based image of masculinity
to commit offenses against the person.

Moreover, the defensive nature of his masculinity
tends to prescribe a specific type of relationship with
the opposite sex. Several researchers report that upper
lower-class adolescents indulge quite regularly in sexual intercourse but that typically there is very little
feeling for or emotional investment in the partner.[42]
The upper lower-class male prefers to remain emotionally distant from girls lest he become dependent
and ultimately humbled. But as a result of his superficial concern, the upper lower-class adolescent can
engage in a wide variety of sexual offenses without
being inhibited by any feeling of sympathy or solici-
tude for the girl. Thus, there is probably some forcible
rape in the upper lower-class, and illicit intercourse is
also likely to be frequent.

The thirst for thrills and novelty so common in this
class also tends to inspire several delinquent patterns
of behavior. For example, there can be little doubt
that auto theft serves as a convenient source of excitement for upper lower-class boys.[43] Moreover, it seems
highly likely that other forms of theft, burglary, and
vandalism are stimulated at times by a desire on the
part of these adolescents to escape boredom.[44] While
beer and alcohol are constant, almost routine, media
of escape, narcotics do not seem to be a frequent route
to thrills and excitement among the members of this
class.[45] It may be that the passivity accompanying the

use of drugs is incompatible with the masculine image held by the members of this class.

All in all, then, the typical upper lower-class youngster is encouraged by the values of his class to resist the efforts of members of the higher classes to manipulate and control him, especially when these attempts imply an invidious comparison between his class and the higher classes. The delinquencies that result under these conditions involve the defiance of duly constituted authority and are regarded by the courts as evidence of the juvenile's ungovernability. He is also frankly encouraged by the upper lower-class image of masculinity to defend his honor with violence when necessary and to indulge his sexual appetites in a variety of ways that are proscribed by law. Thus, he will occasionally be guilty of offenses against the person and such sexual offenses as statutory and forcible rape. Finally, under the prompting of a culturally prescribed yearning for excitement, he will be inclined to indulge in a variety of property offenses like auto theft, petty theft, burglary, and possibly some mild forms of vandalism. Thus, although few upper lower-class adolescents will experiment with every type of delinquent behavior mentioned here, there is definitely an implicit sanctioning of considerable delinquent activity in the upper lower-class.

The Lower Lower-Class

The cultural patterns of the lower lower-class, like those of the other classes, are influenced very heavily by the nature of its function in the community. But unlike the other classes, the lower lower-class has *no* function to perform. Its economic contribution is minimal, since its members are very likely to be unemployed, and it has very little influence either socially or politically in the community. Virtually the only circumstances under which a member of another class will undertake to interrelate with a lower lower-class person is to exploit him for some purpose. Thus, the lower lower-class person is physically in the community, but he is not socially, economically, or politically part of it.

Reflecting the anomalous nature of its position, the cultural patterns of the lower lower-class are founded basically upon anomie and resignation.[46] The typical lower lower-class person has very little confidence in his own ability; he has very little respect or loyalty for the individualism of the higher classes and very little faith that the future will bring any significant change in his present condition. Hence, the cultural patterns that have emerged in the lower lower-class are essentially adjustments to an outcaste status, and they encourage in the main an opportunistic indulgence of one's whims and appetites.[47] Both men and women in this class have abandoned all pretense of conforming to any ethic other than a hedonistic one, and there is very little explicit concern for anything else.

Like the lower middle-class, the lower lower-class does not provide its members with a socially structured framework closely relevant to its function and position in the community. Instead, it merely encourages them to taste the pleasures of life as they can, when and if they can. Unlike the lower middle-class, however, members of the lower lower-class have little fear of community censure; hence, they can follow a nonconformist, self-indulgent path with impunity.

The inspiration that this particular style of life provides for delinquent behavior is rather obvious—it sanctions most forms of acting-out behavior. But since this class does not directly encourage specific qualities or values, it does not directly sanction any particular type of delinquent activity. The lower lower-class does not endorse a vigilant sensitivity on the part of men to criticism, nor does it regard sexual conquests as evidence of masculinity. Instead, the aim of the typical lower lower-class person seems to be one of winning as much physical comfort and pleasure as possible from a rather oppressive and forbidding social milieu. Anything that furthers this end, e.g., money, shrewdness, or criminality, is valued for its usefulness, but only pleasure and comfort are valued for themselves.

The delinquencies of lower lower-class adolescents, therefore, are very likely to assume a self-indulgent, impulsive character. For example, their offenses against property, i.e., thefts and burglaries, will generally be petty in nature and oriented to the relief of more or less pressing immediate needs. They will tend to avoid strong-arm methods against determined, able-bodied store owners, but soft-touches, i.e., women, drunks, and elderly people, will be regularly assaulted and robbed. Moreover, delinquencies involving the illegal use of alcohol and drugs, impulsive, acting-out offenses against the school and police, and most types of sexual offenses will appear quite commonly among the juvenile members of the class.

Their offenses against the person, however, are apt to be proportionately somewhat less common than in the upper lower-class. To be sure, lower lower-class adolescents are as sensitive to criticism as their counterparts in the upper lower-class, but in the lower lower-class the inadequate person is much more accepted and tolerated, and there is not as much pressure upon him to prove his worth repeatedly through combat. There will, however, be considerable violence of the impulsive, acting-out variety, particularly by those adolescents who are physically stronger and larger than the rest. Most generally, these assaultive acts will not result in police or legal action, since they are not usually pressed to dangerous extremes. But because of the ubiquitous presence of dangerous weapons, serious injury to the person will not be uncommon either. Those offenses against the person that do occur among adolescents in the lower lower-class will, however, lack the driving concern for vengeance that is common in the upper lower-class; instead, they will be relatively mild, impulsive, and unpremeditated.

A Social Typology of Delinquency

We have examined in some detail the manner in which two social forces—the cultural themes of social classes and the structural characteristics of cliques and gangs—exercise an influence over the delinquency that appears in a community. Each of these forces operates independently of the other, since the manner in which the gang influences the behavior of its members is not ultimately determined by the nature of its position in the class structure, and vice versa. But the resultant effect of the individual's social field upon his behavior can only be calculated by conceptually interrelating all the distinct forces that compose his social field. Moreover, since we have discussed only a small number of forces, there are only a limited number of ways in which these forces can interrelate to form a social field. Thus, by systematically comparing the nature of the influence that the several social classes exert upon adolescents with the nature of the influence that juvenile gangs and cliques have upon their members, it should be possible to define a series of social fields—each of which is distinctive from the rest, and each of which corresponds to a pattern of delinquent behavior. We are, in other words, now in a position to formulate a social typology of delinquency.

We shall proceed by describing the degree to which informal associations are likely to crystallize into gangs in a given class and how the life style of the class interacts with forces arising in these gangs to shape the behavior of their members. By examining both the influence of class position and gang delinquency upon the individual adolescent, it should be possible to give a more precise description of his behavior than would be possible using either factor separately.

A Mischievous-Indulgent Pattern

There are several reasons why adolescent groups in the upper upper-class are unlikely to mature into highly organized, frankly delinquent gangs. First, upper upper-class adolescents are typically educated in private schools, where the teenage culture has little chance to flourish. The official attitude in these schools is generally not sympathetic toward autonomous, formal clubs; and since the teaching staff is usually quite closely involved with the students, they have little opportunity to evade or defy this policy. Moreover, because vacations periodically interrupt their relationships with one another, the intensity of their relations is usually somewhat less than it might otherwise become. Hence, students in preparatory schools have neither the solidarity among themselves nor the freedom from responsible adult influence to develop highly organized adolescent groups.

Nor do upper upper-class teenagers typically form highly cohesive friendship groups in their home communities. In most communities there is only a limited number of upper upper-class males of roughly the same age to form an adolescent club or gang, and of these, only a portion will be sufficiently compatible to support the formation of a cohesive gang. But even here they will be able to get together only during vacation periods.

It is possible, of course, that some adolescents from the same upper upper-class community will enroll at the same private school and interrelate with one another both at school and at home. But since the major portion of their time is spent at school, where formal adolescent groupings are effectively discouraged, they are probably less likely to form highly solidary groups than the adolescents in other classes. For all these reasons, then, it is not likely that highly organized adolescent clubs or gangs of any sort will develop with any frequency in upper upper-class schools or communities.

This is not to suggest, however, that informal cliques of upper upper-class adolescents are entirely absent in private schools. On the contrary, the austere ethos of these schools, in which each student is rigorously judged in terms of his individual ability, together with the fact that most students in them are separated from their friends and relatives at home, forces many students into close primary relationships with at least a few of their peers.

These cliques are not at first differentiated in terms of centrality or marginality, but gradually, as the students establish their abilities in academic and extracurricular activities, a shuffling tends to occur in which the inept find themselves more or less stuck with each other in marginal cliques. There is no reason to expect these marginal cliques generally to exhibit greater solidarity than the central cliques— indeed, we might anticipate that they would experience considerable anomie. But occasionally, a marginal clique may develop rationalizations, i.e., techniques of neutralization, that explain the ineptitude of its members in terms of someone else's incompetency [48]

Those cliques that can "explain" their marginality in this fashion are probably more stable and solidary than those that cannot on two counts. Whereas their primary purpose is to neutralize the critical judgments of parents and school authorities, these rationalizations also come to symbolize the essential nature of the clique to its members and to nonmembers alike. Thus, the cynical realism characteristic of these techniques often becomes a source of pride to its members—a symbol of their emancipation—while at the same time it comes to represent the clique's marginality to the rest of the school. As the clique perfects its techniques of neutralization, its members become increasingly inured against the warnings of their teachers and increasingly self-conscious of their marginality. The ultimate effect of these rationalizations is to leave the members relatively free to pursue any delinquent pattern of behavior that appears interesting and attractive.

The types of delinquent activity that are appealing in this case depend in part, at least, upon the kinds of values endorsed by the adolescents' parents. In the upper upper-class, therefore, these marginal cliques can be expected to focus primarily upon mischievous theft and property destruction, the indulgence of sexual appetites, and the consumption of quantities of beer and liquor. They do not, however, display much interest in violent, assaultive types of delinquent behavior nor in *systematic* offenses against property.

In most cases, however, these mischievous cliques are not destined to become seriously anti-social gangs.

They are ordinarily under rather close supervision by the school authorities, and before they can become highly structured gangs, they will usually be dispersed. When the school becomes aware of their delinquent tendencies, it can be expected to take steps to suppress these cliques and if necessary to expel the members from the school.

This means, in effect, that the quasi-delinquent clique will have little opportunity to become a highly organized gang and, therefore, that institutionalized delinquency in the upper upper-class will remain relatively unstructured in comparison with that in the other classes. Furthermore, since the clique has little chance to develop a formal authority structure, it has little catalytic affect upon the delinquent tendencies of its members. And because it is dispersed almost before its presence is felt, it never is seriously pressed to defend its legitimacy in the school or community. Hence, the solidarity that its members feel is largely personal in nature, and the clique's sovereignty is relatively weak.

All in all, then, what delinquency there is in the upper upper-class is institutionalized in the marginal cliques that develop in the preparatory schools of this class. But because these cliques are structurally ill-defined and socially alienated from their environment, the moral currents and eddies in the community, as well as the social forces arising directly in the group itself, play a relatively minor role in shaping the delinquent patterns of their members.

An Aggressive-Exploitative Pattern

Institutionalized delinquency among lower upper- and upper middle-class adolescents probably more nearly approaches the gang stage, although once again

when the gang begins to display its delinquent pro-
clivities openly, the community and the parents typically step in with countermeasures to cut short its
existence. Here, however, the community and the
school are less likely to become fully aware of the
nature of the clique before it has actually matured
into a delinquent gang.

High schools in which the graduating class normally
exceeds 60 to 70 students clothe their students in an
anonymity that provides them with considerable freedom from adult control and supervision.[49] A budding
gang, therefore, can establish and consolidate its delinquent tendencies in a large public school to a much
larger degree than its counterpart in a private school
can. Moreover, the highly developed character of the
adolescent society in high schools serving the middle
and upper classes helps to widen the gap between the
adolescents and the adults in the community.[50] In
large metropolitan high schools where the adolescent
society is firmly entrenched, quasi-delinquent groups
and clubs will, thus, have considerable opportunity to
develop quite far in an anti-social direction.[51]

There is some reason, moreover, to expect that the
adolescent society itself will play an important role in
the genesis of certain types of delinquency in these
schools. Adolescent cliques and clubs already have a
highly formal structure, and they also experience some
pressure to defend their legitimacy vis-à-vis rival
groups and school authorities. In addition, they have
a wide variety of nullifying techniques conveniently
at hand that sanction behavior peculiar to the adolescent society while deprecating the values of the larger
society. Thus, the social mechanisms of influence are
already well developed in the adolescent society, and
all that is needed to focus them in a delinquent

direction is a push from the lower upper- and upper middle-class leadership nucleus.

Although the most solidary clubs and cliques in these high schools are generally those involving athletes, it is not very likely that these groups will fall into seriously anti-social patterns. The athletic ability of the members of these cliques forces them into the public spotlight and exposes them to many conventional influences that most adolescents never experience. Thus, high school athletes are an integral part of the community structure and, as such, are in no position to flout or ignore its code of values. Any anti-social tendencies that exist incipiently in the athletic cliques are counterbalanced, therefore, with rather powerful forces of a conventional sort.

A more likely source of delinquent behavior is the cliques of *nonathletic* teenagers. As we have already seen, lower upper- and upper middle-class adolescents are under considerable pressure to demonstrate their worth in individual competition with their peers. But those who are not especially skilled in athletics, i.e., the vast majority, have no particular domain in which they, too, might gain recognition and approval from the community for their individual achievement. Hence, they have no alternative but to depend on their clique for confirmation of their worth and to express their competitive impulses collectively via interclique contests of various sorts.

When a rivalry between two high schools becomes particularly intense, it is usually convenient for the teenagers in these high schools and particularly for those organized into cliques and clubs to express their competitive impulses in a belligerent manner toward each other. The structure of the club gives courage to the fainthearted, and its cultural myths and rationalizations sanctify certain types of assaultive behavior that might otherwise prove disturbing to its members. Hence, there is some reason to expect that high school clubs and fraternities may on occasion launch assaults upon one another and that these interclique fracases may produce rather serious violence.

The experience of conflict and triumph, moreover, often has a curious effect upon the clique. It confirms its legitimacy in much the same way that a victory confirms an athletic team. Thus, as the clique establishes a reputation for routing its opponents, its members feel more valid as males and more worthy as competitors. Their new found self-esteem, however, does not ordinarily stimulate more serious outbursts, since the adolescent society frowns upon unprovoked attacks upon innocent individuals or groups. Instead, it probably results in a more vigorous and confident pursuit of other adolescent values, e.g., drinking and sexual adventures. In the more established teenage clubs, then, a rich tradition of drinking bouts and sexual licentiousness can be expected to accumulate, making the group's influence upon its members even more compelling.

At this point in the clique's development, then, sexual delinquencies, heavy drinking, and assaultive behavior will be a periodic, if not regular, part of its activity; and its organization, traditions, and focus all qualify it as a delinquent gang.[52] To be sure, it is still not recognized as such by the police, the school authorities, or the parents, and even the members do not think of themselves as basically in conflict with society. But it is clear that the clique is anti-social in nature even though delinquency may not be its exclusive orientation.

Should the parents or the school authorities become

aware, at this point, of the actual nature of the gang, they would quickly take steps to disband the members and otherwise disrupt its activities. But the nature of the gang's delinquency is generally either unknown or misinterpreted. Its assaults upon other cliques are generally dismissed as episodic, while its drinking parties are not discouraged as long as they do not result in property destruction or serious auto accidents. Its sexual delinquencies are not common knowledge, although, to be sure, other adolescents generally have some idea of what is going on. Thus, the gang is able to evolve a moderately serious antisocial pattern before the adult community is fully aware of its essential nature.

In the lower upper- and upper middle-classes, however, it is rare that such gangs actually mature into overtly defiant delinquent gangs. The parents have the means to disperse gangs of this type, and when the parents become aware of their nature they usually move quickly. The precipitating event is generally a crisis that arises quite accidentally as the gang follows its customary round of delinquent activity. For example, in the course of its usual pattern of heavy drinking or assaultive contests with competitive cliques, a member may be involved in a serious auto accident, or a major riot may break out involving hundreds of teenagers. The gang's usual pattern of clandestine delinquency, therefore, may precipitate dangerously anti-social behavior, not so much through conscious intent as miscalculation.

Whether intended or not, however, such a crisis forces the lower upper- and upper middle-class community to recognize the delinquent nature of some of its adolescent groups and to take steps to curb them.[53] In effect, this means that the clandestine delinquent pattern of lower upper- and upper middle-class gangs never gets a chance to develop into an openly defiant pattern. When and if it erupts into open delinquency, the community promptly moves to squelch it.

Given these conditions, then, the gang never experiences a serious breach between itself and the rest of the community. Consequently, it is never faced with the necessity of justifying its anti-social nature to its members; and since the question of the gang's legitimacy in the community does not become an important issue, it does not evolve a conflict ideology, i.e., an ideology *frankly* antagonistic toward the rest of the community. In most upper- and middle-class gangs, then, delinquency tends to remain incidental to their major focus, i.e., competition and the acquisition of manhood.

A Criminal Pattern

Since gang delinquency in the upper lower-class has been examined in much greater detail than in any other class, the picture that emerges here can be resolved to an unusual precision. In the lower classes the organization of the community is a much more important factor in shaping the character of its delinquency than in the upper classes. Although the existence of organized crime in the community is not directly relevant to the delinquent patterns of adolescents in higher classes, in the lower class it is of vital significance. As we have already seen, the successful criminal is a man of considerable prestige in the lower-class community, and to the adolescents he is often a symbol of wealth and adventure.[54] Thus, the criminal in the lower-class community often enjoys an influence over local adolescents that few upper-class adults can wield over *their own* youngsters.

One of the factors making organized crime particularly attractive to upper lower-class youngsters is its ability to offer them a career that is exciting, economically rewarding, and highly esteemed in the neighborhood. Adolescents in this class do not generally have ready access to legitimate occupations that can promise as much, and consequently, if they are invited to become a part of a thriving, successful criminal operation, they respond enthusiastically.

Being a part of organized crime is also satisfying to the upper lower-class adolescent because it allows him to express certain deeply held values in a direct and forceful manner. It encourages, for example, a contempt for the conventional, middle-class stratum of the community and permits him to vent some of his resentment toward this class and its institutions. It trains him in the skillful use of violence and accordingly, helps him fulfill his concept of himself as a man. And since it promises adventure, it can prove an effective anodyne for the enervating routine of upper lower-class life. Because the life of the successful criminal is quite consistent with the values of most upper lower-class youngsters, most of them are more than happy to become a part of organized crime.

This means that institutionalized delinquency in upper lower-class communities—where organized crime is firmly established—will tend to be oriented toward offenses that are directly relevant to the operations of the adult criminals.[55] Thus, where organized gambling flourishes, the delinquents will be engaged in violations of gambling laws. Where the adult criminals are engaged in burglaries, robberies, and larcenies, the adolescents will focus their efforts in this area. So, whenever organized crime has been able to develop a profitable operation, under the guidance and tutelage of successful criminals, the adolescents will specialize in those offenses that are directly relevant to this operation.

This close tie-in with organized crime also carries implications for the manner in which the delinquent clique is internally structured. The question of the clique's legitimacy vis-à-vis the rest of the community should lose some of its saliency, since one of the most successful and important elements of the community, the successful criminals in the neighborhood, obviously approves and endorses its existence. These delinquent cliques are not alienated from nor in conflict with the rest of the immediate community, and, for this reason, they are not under great pressure to justify their position in the community.[56]

But if this is the case, the unity and cohesiveness of the clique should suffer. When its legitimacy is obvious, it no longer needs to reiterate its worth to its members, and the strategic significance of the member's allegiance to the clique diminishes. Thus, we can expect that the authority of the clique over the individual should be weakened somewhat by its quasi-legitimate status in the community.

Similarly, we can anticipate that the internal organization of the clique will be relatively informal. The authority of the leaders is subordinate to the adult criminals in the community; hence, their role consists not so much in the exercise of authority as it does in the transmission of authority. What authority they do possess, therefore, probably derives for the most part from their personal skill in areas directly related to the clique's criminal activities, i.e., it is largely charismatic. Thus, with the help and counsel of his criminal friends, the leader senses where the interesting and profitable activities are; and through his relationships with the other members of the clique, he evokes an interest in these kinds of activities. But his authority in the clique is not formal, and it is not compelling for those who are not persuaded by his arguments.[57]

Finally, because the clique is closely aligned with an important group in the community, the need to develop cultural myths that neutralize the moral force of the conventional community is probably somewhat less here than with other delinquent groups. The community is not unalterably and unanimously opposed to these delinquent cliques, and it does not condemn in blanket fashion the group, its members, and its actions. Hence, the individual member is probably not *centrally* conscious of the anti-social character of his behavior, and he probably needs little help in justifying it to himself. Thus, even though these groups are in the mainstream of delinquent life and are perfectly aware of the standard techniques of neutralization used by delinquents, their dependency upon them is probably minimal. As a result, their sense of unity with the entire class of delinquents is probably somewhat weaker than that of other delinquents who share these techniques more profoundly.[58]

For these reasons, then, the type of delinquency that springs up in stable, upper lower-class neighborhoods in which organized crime has taken firm root does not ordinarily give rise to highly structured and focused gangs. Rather, the cliques that develop are loosely structured, and, in comparison with some other delinquent cliques and gangs, relatively powerless to shape the behavior of their members. The dominant factor here seems to be the values and perspectives of the major adult criminal groups in the community. The delinquent clique is thus more a collection of like-minded and similarly oriented youngsters than anything else. Since there are many immediate advantages associated with membership in the clique, it is a privilege to belong. Those who cannot pass muster are not admitted, whereas those who prove to be incompetent or otherwise unworthy are eliminated. Hence, the authority of the clique derives chiefly from the close congruence that exists between the values of its members and the objectives of the clique. It is, therefore, more nearly a guild than a gang or a team.

A Fighting Pattern

Although the fully developed fighting gang is probably less common that the criminally oriented gang, it is certainly more prominent in the nation's newspapers and criminologic literature.

Several observers report that the emergence of the fighting gang is related to the degree of disorganization found in the community.[59] When the adolescents are largely cut off from meaningful contact with adults in the community, they are free to follow any value system that is convenient. In the upper lower-class this means, in particular, that adolescent cliques will tend to be rather sensitive to questions of honor and that they will be ready to settle disputes with force.

And, moreover, where this preoccupation with honor and revenge is coupled with a climate of challenge and conflict in the community, an ordinary upper lower-class clique is likely to be transformed into a vicious, marauding fighting gang. An overly zealous enforcement of the law, for example, may goad the clique as a whole into vengeful retaliation against the police. Or a relatively minor dispute between two individuals may escalate into a bitter feud between their respective cliques.

But regardless of the initial spark, the eruption of violent conflict works a fundamental change upon the clique.[60] First, it calls into serious question, as nothing else can, the legitimacy of the clique in the larger community. A chronic dispute with the police tends to isolate the clique and to confirm its illegal status. A serious feud with other cliques forces it to meet their challenge not only with force but also with protestations of its own moral superiority. Thus, open conflict forces the clique into greater moral independence and self-sufficiency.

Its isolation means, further, that the members will become especially dependent on the clique and its peculiar moral code for determining their course of action. A "siege mentality" grows within the clique in which the members become preoccupied with their allegiance to the clique and its values and sharply conscious of their estrangement from other groups in the community.[61] Thus, open conflict produces a closely integrated clique in which the loyalty of its members is devoted largely to the clique and its moral code.[62]

This strong sense of solidarity, along with its rivalry with other groups, tends also to impose a highly formal authority structure upon the group, in which the leader's functions are twofold: to represent symbolically the group and its virtues to the other members; and to provide wise and effectual counsel in times of crisis. Thus, the leader must be worthy of the members' admiration, and he must be alert and appreciative of the possibilities in specific situations.[63] With the emergence of a formal leader, of course, the discipline of the clique increases, and its ability to sanction and otherwise shape the behavior of its members grows significantly.

At this point in its development, the clique has become a full-fledged gang with a clear identity and an internal structure. Moreover, as its isolation from the rest of the community becomes complete and its violence becomes wanton, the members become increasingly dependent upon the cultural myths that seem to explain and sanction their more violent outbursts. Their sense of separation from the conventional world grows and their use of techniques of neutralization symbolizes and confirms their membership in an anti-social stratum of the community.

The eruption of violence among upper lower-class cliques tends, therefore, to induce a skein of adjustments that ultimately results in a few of these ordinary cliques becoming highly structured, cohesive fighting gangs. The emergence of the fighting gang may be facilitated by the sense of status-frustration that is often felt by the upper lower-class youngsters, as Cloward and Ohlin suggest.[64] But we need not make this kind of assumption to explain the significance of violence for the upper lower-class clique.

The respect that the typical member of this class has for violence and its uses is sufficient reason to anticipate periodic outbursts in the ordinary round of his daily life. Since violence by its nature tends to inflame and arouse counterviolence, once it is expressed it tends to set in motion a chain reaction that often culminates in felonious assault and more serious crimes. Thus, where upper lower-class adolescents tend to form themselves into highly solidary cliques and where relationships between these cliques are competitive, we can expect fighting gangs to emerge.

These conditions are most frequently met when two distinct lower-class ethnic groups live in close proximity, with considerable prejudice and ill will flowing between them. The bitterness of the adults in the community means that teenage cliques in the area will tend to form along ethnic lines and that their attitudes will tend to be competitive. If the outgroup is inclined to reciprocate in kind—if its image of masculinity requires that all insults be avenged—any incidental dispute between members of the rival ethnic groups could touch off an interclique feud and ultimately foster the development of fighting gangs in both camps.

The members of the gangs need not all be upper lower-class adolescents, once the cycle has been set in motion. Indeed, many lower lower-class boys may use the gang as a means of upward mobility into the upper lower-class and its clique network. But it is apparent that a conception of the male as a vigilant and vengeful person is a necessary precondition for the *emergence* of fighting gangs, and the lower lower-class does not endorse this conception of masculinity as strongly as the upper lower-class does.

The Puerto Ricans in New York City may appear to be exceptional here, but in reality they tend to confirm this analysis. Although their position in New York City is undoubtedly lower lower-class, they continue to endorse many aspects of Spanish culture, including an image of the male as vigorous, proud, and sensitive to questions of honor. Any violence directed against the Puerto Ricans, therefore, can be expected to kindle a spirited reply; and where Puerto Ricans invade a neighborhood of upper lower-class native Americans, we might expect to find considerable gang warfare. Indigenous lower lower-class adolescents living in inner-city slums, however, can be expected to accept the indignities and depredations of their upper lower-class neighbors more passively and less violently.[65]

A Theft Pattern

Most typically, however, the upper lower-class clique confronts neither a belligerent challenge from other groups in the community nor a highly organized adult criminal stratum. The most typical delinquent pattern in the upper lower-class, therefore, is probably neither of the types we have discussed thus far, but rather a third type, which is defined basically in terms of the values of this class.

We have already seen that, in addition to an intense concern for masculinity, the values of the upper lower-class lay particular stress on finding diversions from the upper lower-class round of life and on resisting the efforts of authority figures who are attempting to control and channel their behavior. Thus, besides the occasional fights in which boys in this class engage to preserve their honor, they also probably indulge in a wide variety of sexual activities; seek excitement in minor offenses against property; consume considerable amounts of beer, liquor, and wine; and resist the efforts of teachers, police, and others to modify their behavior through threat or coercion. As in the other classes, therefore, a considerable amount of delinquency can be anticipated when teenage groups in the upper lower-class simply conform to the time-honored values of their class.

To be sure, a seriously anti-social gang might emerge from this pattern in the same way that the fighting gang emerges from a pattern of juvenile conflict. If the community comes to focus on the clique and condemns it as unworthy, it may harden in its delinquent pattern and become self-consciously defiant toward the community. Moreover, should it become overtly anti-social, its delinquency is likely to focus upon offenses against property, since these are especially annoying to the larger community. Its sexual delinquencies and its violations of the liquor laws are not so irritating as its depredations against property. Hence, when it seeks to repudiate the community, the gang is forced to resort to vandalism and theft.

The solidarity of such a gang probably approaches that of the fighting gang. As the gang becomes isolated, its sense of alienation grows and the members become more dependent upon each other for moral support. Moreover, as the gang becomes frankly delinquent, the members are forced to adopt the techniques of neutralization that all delinquents resort to, and their sense of community with other delinquents is thereby increased. It is conceivable, therefore, that the same forces that foster fighting gangs in working-class communities may also begin to operate here as well and fashion a defiant adolescent gang that expresses its repudiation of the community primarily in offenses against property.

But the likelihood of a working-class clique being transformed in this fashion into a seriously anti-social gang is not great. The community does not ordinarily seize upon the activities of these cliques and condemn them as immoral and unworthy until they have progressed to really serious proportions. The ordinary sexual delinquencies of male working-class adolescents are not strongly disapproved, and their drinking escapades are not regarded as especially noteworthy. As long as their offenses against property do not become serious, the community does not consider the clique as anything other than a normal working-class group of boys. Its delinquent activities are evaluated in this context, and for this reason the clique is not regarded as seriously delinquent even though it does embark upon a wide variety of anti-social activities. Thus, when working-class adolescents are not confronted with unusual conditions in their environment, they tend to engage in a pattern of mild delinquency that essentially reflects the values of their class.[66] And most generally, they do not mature into seriously delinquent gangs.

In sum, then, the type of institutionalized delinquency that develops in the upper lower-class depends both upon the value-system peculiar to this class and upon the organization of the larger community. When organized crime plays an important role in a solidary community, the delinquent cliques that emerge will tend to commit offenses that are encouraged by professional criminals in the area. The structure of these cliques tends to be informal and loosely defined, and their function is to orient the adolescent toward attractive career opportunities in the adult criminal world and to cultivate the attitudes and skills that are relevant to this world.

When the community is more disorganized, the adolescents will have fewer meaningful relationships with adults, and the delinquent cliques will tend to be governed more diffusely by the prevailing values of their upper lower-class members. If the neighborhood is also racked with racial or ethnic hatreds, the gangs that develop will be oriented toward violent conflict and their organization will tend to be formal, disciplined, and cohesive.

A Pattern of Disorganized Acting-Out

It is unlikely that highly structured, delinquent groups will make their appearance in the lower lower-class with any frequency. Since the anomic apathy of lower lower-class adults extends to the adolescents as well, their ability to submit to the organization and discipline of a highly structured group is not great. Their peer-groups are, thus, spontaneous and informal, while at the same time they are unstable and impermanent. The members of these groups are not under appreciable pressure to participate in the group's activities or to adjust their egocentric patterns to its discipline. Hence, the anarchy of lower lower-class life is also the dominant pattern in its adolescent peer-groups.

Contributing indirectly to the relatively informal, unstable structure of these groups is the indifference felt by most lower lower-class adults for the adolescents of this class. Delinquent adolescents, i.e., the vast majority, are not strongly condemned for their delinquent behavior; and consequently, they are not under unusual pressure to justify the existence of their antisocial cliques in the community. Their existence may be a source of concern for the police, but the police do not exercise moral authority in the community, and their reprimands and warnings are no more meaningful to the denizens of inner-city slums than the recriminations of Mao Tse-tung. Thus, the typical lower lower-class adolescent does not regard his participation in a delinquent clique as of any particular moral significance, and the clique does not typically evoke among its members a strong allegiance to its values and activities.

This is not to say that the lower lower-class adolescent is unaware of the abhorrence with which the rest of the community regards his class or that he does not react to this abhorrence. Rather, I am suggesting that since his membership in a delinquent clique does not significantly alter this abhorrence, the illegal nature of his clique activities does not increase his sense of estrangement beyond what he already feels as an individual. Therefore, the delinquent cliques in this class are not likely to adopt a siege mentality, and they do not typically foster among their members an unusual loyalty to the clique or a resentment toward other groups or cliques.

The lower lower-class adolescent is, of course, deeply aware of his outcast status in the community; and consequently, his dependence upon culturally based rationalizations justifying the behavior and position of his caste is considerable. He shares with the rest of his caste the conviction that the techniques of neutralization mentioned above are valid and factual, and he explains his frequent violations of the community's legal and moral code largely in terms of them. His use of these cultural rationalizations, however, is not a reflection of his delinquent identity so much as it is of his membership in the lower lower-class. These techniques serve mainly to perpetuate in his consciousness an awareness that his *class* is morally distinct and reprehensible in the eyes of the community.

Because of the generally chaotic nature of these adolescent cliques, their influence upon the delinquent patterns of their members is insignificant compared with that of some of the cliques in the other classes. Hence, the delinquent cliques of the lower lower-class will indulge in much the same kinds of delinquent offenses that lower lower-class individuals do. In other words, most forms of acting-out behavior —petty theft, assault, robbery, and sexual offenses of virtually every description—will be quite common. Moreover, in the larger metropolitan areas these cliques can also be expected to experiment with esoteric forms of sensual indulgence—narcotics for example. Their use of narcotics, however, probably represents an attempt to exploit one more method of enjoying pleasure more than it does a retreat from a defeating, frustrating environment as Cloward and Ohlin suggest.[67]

The resigned, apathetic character of life in this class probably rules out the frequent appearance of cliques and gangs that aggressively provoke conflicts with other adolescent cliques in the neighborhood. They may be obliged to defend themselves against other, more aggressive, gangs, but organized violence is not their particular inclination or skill. Rather than vigilantly defending their honor in the face of attacks from alien groups, they would prefer to melt into their surroundings and avoid such issues altogether.

In sum, then, illegal behavior is an integral part of lower lower-class culture and not an autonomous pattern unique to delinquents. Although the adolescent cliques that develop in this class are likely to display a wide variety of delinquent activities, they are not likely to evolve a rigid internal structure or a close discipline over their members. The impulsive individualism characteristic of the lower lower-class as a whole is, therefore, the prevailing theme among its adolescents as well.

Conclusion

I have sought in this analysis to suggest several ways in which distinctive social forces enter the adolescent's situation and encourage specific types of delinquent actions. I have examined the manner in which class position structures the delinquent patterns of adolescents, and I have indicated four ways in which his membership in a delinquent group affects a teenager's behavior. These forces, although distinct in their development, interrelate in the social field of the community to confront its members with characteristic social situations. And by systematically examining how these forces interrelate, it is possible to identify six distinctive patterns of delinquent behavior: an upper upper-class pattern of mischievous-indulgence; a lower upper- and upper middle-class pattern of aggressive-exploitation; three upper lower-class patterns, a criminally oriented, a conflict oriented, and a theft pattern; and a pattern of disorganized acting-out delinquency in the lower lower class. A schematic diagram of this typology is presented in Table One below.

Although this typology is defined primarily in terms of social forces that positively shape the behavior of adolescents, it was also necessary to consider forces that act mainly to inhibit delinquent behavior: the ability of the family and community to control their adolescents. The degree to which delinquency establishes itself in a community depends not only upon the community pressures inducing it, but also upon the ease with which the community is able to mount counteractive measures to disperse delinquent cliques and gangs.[68]

One of the major differences between the delinquent patterns of the upper and middle classes and those of the lower class is the relative effectiveness with which conventional groups—parents and school authorities—deal with emerging delinquent groups

TABLE ONE A SOCIAL TYPOLOGY OF DELINQUENCY

Type	Social Structure	Degree of Alienation from Community	Delinquent Patterns	Class Origins of Members
Mischievous-Indulgent	Weakly organized, clique structures at best.	Somewhat alienated from conventional peers and adults.	Delinquent exploits exhibit style and taste, indulgent toward appetites.	Primarily upper upper-class youths, upwardly mobile lower status youths.
Aggressive-Exploitative	Well organized into clubs and gangs of adolescent society.	Delinquent activities are unknown to conventional adults, minimally alienated.	Emphasis upon proving oneself through sexual, drinking, and physical competition.	Lower upper-, upper middle-class, and upwardly mobile youths.
Criminal	Loosely organized in terms of clique structure.	Well integrated with criminal adults, not rejected by most conventional adults in immediate neighborhood.	Emphasis upon skill in criminal techniques, pursuit of criminal activities related to adult criminal practices.	Upper lower- and upwardly mobile lower lower-class youngsters.
Fighting	Very well organized with formal positions and strong solidarity.	Condemned and despised by immediate community, high degree of alienation.	Major emphasis upon attitudes and skills needed in physical combat.	Upper lower- and upwardly mobile lower lower-class youngsters.
Theft	Loosely organized in terms of friendship cliques.	Not rejected by immediate community, not seriously alienated.	Indulgence of appetites, theft for excitement, assaultive when challenged, vandalism toward schools.	Upper lower- and upwardly mobile lower lower-class youngsters.
Disorganized Acting-Out	Very loosely organized, little structure at all.	Behavior not easily distinguished from normal adult patterns.	Indulgence of appetites, impulsive assaults, thefts and use of narcotics.	Lower lower-class.

when they appear. In the upper classes it is generally a simple matter for the parents and school authorities to disperse delinquent cliques by isolating their members before their delinquent activities can grow to serious proportions. But in the lower classes the parents and school authorities find it quite impossible to follow a similar course, and consequently, in the lower classes delinquency is sometimes allowed to build to a level that finally forces the police and the courts to intervene. Unfortunately, however, the police and the courts serve mainly to confirm the delinquent tendencies of these cliques with the result that delinquency becomes firmly established in the lower-class community. The serious anti-social patterns of the lower class, then, may not represent the influence of extraordinary deviancy pressures so much as the difficulty these communities face in suppressing delinquent groups.

Whether we are considering positive or negative factors in delinquency, it is apparent that the forces entering the social field of a community do not interact in a simple, mechanical fashion to create delinquency-inducing situations. Rather, they augment and neutralize one another in terms of their significance for each other to produce situations that their individual qualities could never suggest. The fighting gang, for example, cannot be explained simply in terms of the inclinations of upper lower-class youths to defend their honor violently. Instead, it must be viewed as a result of the peculiar significance that occasional violence has for the internal structure of groups and for their relations with other groups in the community.

Where the forces at work in a community interrelate sympathetically in this fashion, we can expect that the resultant social situations will be particularly enduring and stable. The sociologist's task is to identify these harmonically related forces by systematically examining the implications that the forces in a social field contain for each other. The construction of a social typology of delinquency must begin, therefore, with the identification of the social forces that are relevant to delinquency, and it must end with a determination of the ways in which these basic forces interact to yield relatively stable social situations.

I obviously have not exhausted the full range of social forces that are relevant to delinquent behavior, and accordingly, the social typology put forth here is not definitive in either an extensive or an intensive sense. Nevertheless, when other social forces that are relevant to delinquent behavior are identified, it should be a simple matter to relate them systematically to the types we have already derived. And when they have all been ultimately discovered, a definitive social typology of delinquency will be possible that includes all the types that are permissible in terms of social theory and that describes each of these types in fine detail.

NOTES

[1] See Don Martindale, *The Nature and Types of Sociological Theory* (Boston: Houghton Mifflin, 1960), Parts Three, Four, and Six for a description of these theoretical viewpoints.

[2] Fritz Redl and David Wineman, *The Aggressive Child* (New York: Free Press, 1957), pp. 145–56.

[3] Gresham Sykes and David Matza, "Techniques of Neutralization: A Theory of Delinquency," *American Sociological Review*, Vol. 22, No. 6 (December, 1957), pp. 664–70.

[4] Charles B. Spaulding, "Cliques, Gangs, and Networks," *Sociology and Social Research*, Vol. 32, No. 6 (July–August, 1948), pp. 928–37.

[5] Arthur J. Rogers, *Reaching the Fighting Gang* (New York: New York City Youth Board, 1960), pp. 44–45, 51–55. See also Lewis Yablonsky, *The Violent Gang* (New York: Macmillan, 1962), pp. 206–21.

[6] See the incident involving Duke described by Fred L. Strodtbeck and James F. Short in their article "An Explanation of Gang Action," *Social Problems*, Vol. 12, No. 2 (Fall, 1964), pp. 129–31.

[7] Spaulding, "Cliques," p. 929.

[8] Solomon Kobrin, "Sociological Aspects of the Development of a Street Corner Group: An Exploratory Study," *American Journal of Orthopsychiatry*, Vol. 31, No. 4 (July, 1961), p. 688. See also Albert K. Cohen, *Delinquent Boys* (New York: Free Press, 1955), pp. 132–34.

[9] Cohen, *Delinquent Boys*, pp. 109–19; and Frank Riessman, *The Culturally Deprived Child* (New York: Harper & Row, 1962), pp. 16–24.

[10] Frederic M. Thrasher, *The Gang*, 2d ed. (Chicago: University of Chicago Press, 1936), pp. 30–32.

[11] Richard A. Cloward and Lloyd E. Ohlin, *Delinquency and Opportunity* (New York: Free Press, 1960), pp. 144–60.

[12] *Ibid.*, pp. 161–71.

[13] *Ibid.*, pp. 171–78.

[14] *Ibid.*, pp. 178–86.

[15] Walter B. Miller, "Lower Class Culture as a Generating Milieu of Gang Delinquency," *Journal of Social Issues*, Vol. 14, No. 1 (April, 1958), pp. 5–19.

[16] David Matza and Gresham Sykes, "Juvenile Delin-

quency and Subterranean Values," *American Sociological Review,* Vol. 26, No. 5 (Oct., 1961), pp. 720–32; and Edwin H. Sutherland, *White Collar Crime* (New York: Holt, Rinehart & Winston, 1961).

17 W. Lloyd Warner, *The Social Life of a Modern Community* (New Haven: Yale University Press, 1941).

18 E. Digby Baltzell, *Philadelphia Gentlemen* (New York: Free Press, 1958), pp. 52–64.

19 For an interesting account of this pattern, see E. Digby Baltzell's *The Protestant Establishment* (New York: Random House, 1964).

20 Nathaniel Burt, *The Perennial Philadelphians* (Boston: Little, Brown, 1963), pp. 32–76, 584–88.

21 A. B. Hollingshead, *Elmtown's Youth* (New York: Science Editions, 1961), pp. 84–90.

22 At a recent football game between Harvard and Holy Cross, a Harvard student dressed in clerical garb elaborately bestowed his "blessing" upon the team at the half-time huddle in full view of the crowd.

23 The Southampton incident is reported in *The New York Times,* September 4, 1963, p. 41. For a picture story of the same incident, see *Life Magazine,* September 20, 1963.

24 Genevieve Knupfer and Robin Room, "Drinking in a Metropolitan Community," *Social Problems,* Vol. 12, No. 2 (Fall, 1964), pp. 224–40.

25 Hollingshead, *Elmtown's Youth,* pp. 90–95.

26 John R. Seeley, R. A. Sim, and E. W. Loosley, *Crestwood Heights* (New York: Basic Books, 1956), p. 120.

27 Hollingshead, *Elmtown's Youth,* p. 91.

28 James S. Coleman, *The Adolescent Society* (New York: Free Press, 1961), pp. 306–9.

29 *Ibid.,* pp. 103–10. See also Hollingshead, *Elmtown's Youth,* pp. 204–42.

30 Coleman, *Adolescent Society,* pp. 27–57. Talcott Parsons was one of the first to identify these patterns among

adolescents in his essay, "Age and Sex in the Social Structure of the United States," *American Sociological Review,* Vol. 7, No. 6 (1942), pp. 604–16.

[31] Howard L. and Barbara G. Myerhoff, "Field Observations of Middle Class 'Gangs'," *Social Forces,* Vol. 42, No. 3 (March, 1964), pp. 328–35.

[32] It is interesting in this regard that the *highest* rates of illegitimacy among white females between the ages of fifteen and nineteen occur in upper-status suburban communities. See Sidney Goldstein and Kurt B. Mayer, "Illegitimacy, Residence, and Status," *Social Problems,* Vol. 12, No. 4 (Spring, 1965), pp. 428–36.

[33] Warner, *Social Life,* pp. 435–39.

[34] C. Wright Mills, *White Collar* (New York: Oxford University Press, 1951), pp. 224–28.

[35] *Ibid.,* pp. 254–58.

[36] Hollingshead, *Elmtown's Youth,* pp. 95–102.

[37] *Ibid.,* pp. 95, 102–3.

[38] S. M. Miller and Frank Riessman, "The Working Class Subculture: A New View," *Social Problems,* Vol. IX, No. 1 (Summer, 1961), pp. 86–97.

[39] Walter B. Miller, "Gang Delinquency," pp. 16–17, and Nathan Hurvitz, "Marital Strain in the Blue Collar Family," in Arthur B. Shostak and William Gomberg, eds., *Blue Collar World* (Englewood Cliffs: Prentice-Hall, 1964), pp. 92–109.

[40] Walter B. Miller, "Gang Delinquency," p. 6; S. M. Miller and Frank Riessman, "Working Class," p. 94; and Herbert J. Gans, *The Urban Villagers* (New York: Free Press, 1962), pp. 28–32.

[41] Walter B. Miller, "Aggression in a Boy's Street-Corner Group," *Psychiatry,* Vol. 24, No. 4 (November, 1961), pp. 283–98.

[42] Arnold Green, "The 'Cult of Personality' and Sexual Relations," *Psychiatry,* Vol. 4, No. 3 (August, 1941), pp. 343–48; Clark Vincent, "Ego Involvement in Sexual Rela-

tions: Implications for Research in Illegitimacy," *American Journal of Sociology*, Vol. LXV, No. 3 (November, 1959), pp. 287–95; and Hurvitz, "Marital Strain," pp. 101–2.

43 Erwin Schepses, "Boys Who Steal Cars," *Federal Probation*, Vol. 25, No. 1 (March, 1961), pp. 56–62.

44 Marshall B. Clinard and Andrew L. Wade, "Juvenile Vandalism," in Ruth Cavan, ed., *Readings in Juvenile Delinquency* (Philadelphia: Lippincott, 1964), pp. 220–26.

45 Isidor Chein, "Narcotics Use Among Juveniles," *Social Work*, Vol. 1, No. 1 (April, 1956), pp. 50–60.

46 Michael Harrington, *The Other America* (New York: Macmillan, 1963), pp. 133–37.

47 Michael Schwartz and George Henderson, "The Culture of Unemployment," in Shostak and Gomberg, *Blue Collar*, pp. 459–68; and Herman Lantz, "Resignation, Industrialization, and the Problem of Social Change," in *ibid.*, pp. 258–70.

48 A careful reading of J. D. Salinger's *Catcher in the Rye* reveals that the hero, Holden Caulfield, used these same kinds of rationalizations in explaining his inability to accept the routine of several private schools. See also David Winter, *et al.*, "The Classic Personal Style," *Journal of Abnormal and Social Psychology*, Vol. 67, No. 3 (1963), pp. 254–65.

49 Roger W. Barker and Paul V. Gump, *Big School, Small School* (Stanford: Stanford University Press, 1964), pp. 132–35.

50 *Ibid.*, pp. 113–14.

51 This may explain why there is proportionately more delinquency among the upper classes in high schools dominated by these classes. See Albert J. Reiss and Albert L. Rhodes, "Delinquency and Social Class Structure," *American Sociological Review*, Vol. 26, No. 5 (October, 1961), pp. 720–32.

52 Ralph W. England, "Theory of Middle Class Juvenile Delinquency," *Journal of Criminal Law, Criminology, and*

Police Science, Vol. 50, No. 4 (December, 1949), pp. 535–40.

53 The kind of nightmare that such communities go through when they finally awaken to the nature of their problem is illustrated by the experience of Darien, Connecticut, following the death of a prominent family's daughter in an automobile accident in June, 1964. *Time Magazine,* October 16, 1964, pp. 61–62.

54 See also Irving Spergel, *Racketville, Slumtown, and Haulberg* (Chicago: University of Chicago Press, 1964), pp. 114–17, 145.

55 *Ibid.,* pp. 30–38.

56 *Ibid.,* pp. 129–30, 144–45.

57 This is not to suggest that the leader's power over his followers is not substantial. His power derives in the main from his personal skills and qualities, but since the group is loosely structured, the basis for a leader's authority is less than it might otherwise be. Spergel reports that the solidarity of this gang is most often based upon personal friendship and kinship ties and not upon the leader's authority. See *ibid.,* pp. 31, 71.

58 Spergel indicates that members of these gangs are on equal terms with delinquents and nondelinquents in their neighborhoods. See *ibid.,* p. 79.

59 Solomon Kobrin, "The Conflict of Values in Delinquency Areas," *American Sociological Review,* Vol. 16, No. 5 (October, 1951), pp. 653–61; and Spergel, *Racketville,* pp. 19–21.

60 Frank Tannenbaum, *Crime and the Community* (Boston: Ginn, 1938), pp. 66–81. Spergel also suggests that conflict is a factor in the emergence of most gangs. See Spergel, *Racketville,* p. 66.

61 Arthur J. Rogers, *Reaching the Fighting Gang* (New York: New York City Youth Board, 1960), pp. 42–44.

62 Spergel suggests that the structure of the criminal and fighting gangs is more stable than that of the theft-oriented gang. See Spergel, *Racketville,* p. 67.

63 Rogers, *Fighting Gang,* pp. 51–55.

64 Richard A. Cloward and Lloyd E. Ohlin, *Delinquency and Opportunity* (New York: Free Press, 1960), pp. 175–78.

65 Spergel presents evidence that fighting gangs are most common among the Puerto Ricans in New York and that those Puerto Ricans who are caught up in fighting gangs are *not* generally in the lowest stratum in the community. See Spergel, *Racketville,* pp. 2, 6.

66 Spergel indicates that cliques engaging primarily in theft are relatively informal and unstructured. See *ibid.,* pp. 67, 72, 76.

67 Cloward and Ohlin, *Delinquency,* pp. 183–84.

68 See Walter C. Reckless, *The Crime Problem,* 3d ed. (New York: Appleton-Century-Crofts, 1961), pp. 335–59 for an attempt to develop a theory of containment.

CHAPTER 5

A Psychological Typology
of Delinquency

Probably no theoretical viewpoint has proved so fertile for the genesis of typologies of delinquency as the systematic study of the human mind. In the last 50 years there have been at least a dozen attempts to derive a typology of delinquency or criminality by appealing to psychological theory, and among those most active in this regard have certainly been the students of Freudian psychology. Psychoanalytic theory is, of course, rather well systematized and lends itself readily to the formulation of typologies. Moreover, psychologists of a psychoanalytic persuasion have been drawn into the firsthand study of deviant behavior by the courts and correctional institutions, and they have thereby gained much valuable experience to guide their theoretical speculations. It should come as no surprise, therefore, that until very recently the typological study of delinquency was carried forward largely by psychoanalytic psychologists.

The main task of a psychological typology of delinquency and crime is to chart the motivational, emotional, and attitudinal complexes behind deviant behavior. Certainly, some types of delinquents and criminals follow the patterns they do because they feel compelled by inwardly rising urges to commit illegal acts, and it is the task of the psychologist to identify how these impulses emerge in the individual's psychological field and structure his life-space. Not every compelling urge has a psychological origin nor can every deviant act be traced back to the psychological field, but some can; and it is the office of psychology to identify the forces in the psychological field that are responsible for deviant motives and attitudes in the life-space and to indicate how these in turn ultimately contribute to deviant behavior.

A second problem that the psychologist must confront in formulating a typology of delinquency is that of explaining why the psychological field of a delinquent impels him to enact his inner struggles in public with the community as his audience instead of suffering his anxieties and fears in private as the vast majority do. The psychologist must establish what it is in the delinquent that dictates an alloplastic solution to his problems instead of a neurotic, autoplastic response. These are the questions that psychological theory is peculiarly fitted to resolve, and in this chapter we shall look rather closely at some of the answers different scholars have provided.

One of the first, of course, to apply psychological theory to criminal behavior was Freud himself. In attempting to trace the differences among several different types of patients that he regularly encountered in his practice, Freud commented very briefly on two criminal types. As his experience in treating psychoneurosis grew, Freud observed that some of his patients seemed to become most troubled when they had least reason to do so, i.e., their symptoms became most pronounced just when their deepest wishes were about to be fulfilled. And among these unfortunates

were some who felt compelled to commit easily de-
tected crimes so that they might be punished.[1] Their
punishment, Freud concluded, helped to assuage an
unconscious guilt that had developed originally in a
serious Oedipal conflict in childhood.

Later, in 1932, Freud also mentioned another type
of criminal that subsequently has received considerable attention in the criminologic literature. In describing how the libido develops, he suggested that the
narcissistic type, in which the libido has invested
much of its energy in the ego, is particularly prone to
criminality because of its freedom from close attachments with peers and from residual identifications
with parents, teachers, or nurses.[2] Freud failed to
expand upon these insights because he was not primarily interested in criminology, his contributions in
this area being largely incidental to a more general
concern with psychoanalytic theory.

Alexander's and Staub's Typology of Criminality

Alexander and Staub, however, did pursue these
initial insights further; and on the basis of Freud's
theory of the mind, they were able to identify two
broad classes of criminality: chronic criminality and
accidental criminality.[3] The chronic criminal can be
recognized by the fact that the sources of his deviancy
are found in his own psychic apparatus, whereas the
crimes of the accidental criminal arise primarily in the
vagaries of an unkind fate. It was the chronic criminal
that stirred the imaginations of Alexander and Staub,
and accordingly, they differentiated five distinct types
of such criminals.

The first type includes those mental defectives, alco-
holics, and drug addicts whose faculties are so be-
numbed by their pathologies that they are literally

unable to control themselves. Their problem seems to stem from a disabled ego that allows relatively weak unconscious needs to gain expression in behavior. Since their criminality is based upon the debilitating effect of their organic or toxic pathologies, they might be described as *organic or toxic criminals.*[4]

Another type of chronic criminal mentioned by Alexander and Staub exhibits a somewhat greater ability to sublimate unconscious needs, but because the ego occasionally relaxes its vigilance, unconscious needs still break through into consciousness and overt behavior. Depending upon the mechanisms responsible for the lapse, two distinct types can be distinguished.[5] We have, on the one hand, the *compulsive* or *symptomatic criminal* whose criminality appears as an alien pattern in an otherwise normal personality. The criminal is surprised and embarrassed by his behavior and gives in to it only reluctantly. A periodic compulsion wells up within him so strongly that the ego is overwhelmed and momentarily swept along in compliance with the demands of the id. On the other hand, we have the *neurotic acting-out criminal,* who also becomes a criminal as a result of powerful unconscious impulses, but whose ego is much more willing to launch unconscious needs into action. For example, the ego may seek criminality as a way of attracting punishment so that a lingering unconscious sense of guilt might be assuaged, or through rationalizations the ego may succeed in misrepresenting to itself the real nature of the repressed wishes in the unconscious. In either case, however, the ego is actively enlisted in the service of the unconscious needs.

A fourth type of chronic criminal is called by Alexander and Staub the *normal criminal.*[6] In this type the ego and superego are both solidly behind criminal behavior and pursue it as assiduously as any artisan pursues his craft. This type results when the superego itself identifies with criminal standards and admonishes the ego to pursue a criminal course, even though it is deviant from the standpoint of the general community. The fifth type, the *genuine criminal,* is also wholeheartedly involved in his criminal exploits, but only because the distinction between his unconscious and ego processes has never been clearly established in his personality.[7] His superego is inchoate, and consequently, when environmental conditions permit, there is very little in the id that is forbidden direct expression in behavior. The ego is sufficient to its task, but since the superego has never fully matured, few if any impulses need to be repressed in the individual's development.

Criminals in the second broad category, accidental criminality, are not governed so powerfully by their internal compulsions; instead, they are more likely to become criminal in response to unusual environmental pressures and demands.[8] To be sure, the *mistaken criminal* who after great strain becomes careless and causes serious injury or damage is giving vent to unconscious wishes just as much as the compulsive criminal, but only after the ego has been first weakened by unusual demands from the environment. And by the same token, the *situational criminal,* who momentarily behaves criminally when confronted with an intense crisis, is also provoked by external events, even though the actual nature of his reaction again depends upon the state of his ego and unconscious. The principal difference, therefore, between the chronic and the accidental criminal seems to be that in the former the trigger to the criminal behavior is intrapsychic, whereas in the latter the original stimulus arises in the environment. Both types of criminality, however, are guided in their behavior by the basic nature of their psychic structure.

In substance, then, Alexander and Staub have derived six different types of criminals by appealing to psychoanalytic theory. All six of these types—the organic and/or toxic criminal, the symptomatic criminal, the neurotic acting-out criminal, the genuine criminal, the mistaken criminal, and the situational criminal—are viewed as behaving criminally in response to the distinctive manner in which their unconscious needs interrelate with their egos and their superegos. All these types are certainly responding to circumstances in their environment—but these circumstances function primarily to trigger criminality; they do not *shape* it.

A seventh type, the *normal criminal,* is not guided essentially by psychological processes in his behavior. This type has successfully internalized the standards of his environment and is quite able to sublimate most of his unconscious needs in behavior. The only problem is that the proscriptions and prescriptions to which he is conforming are themselves criminal; hence, what is moral to him is criminal in the eyes of the larger community. The normal criminal is primarily guided in his behavior by culturally defined standards; and for this reason, his inner dynamics cannot be considered as the essential factor shaping his behavior. Certainly psychological processes underlie his behavior, and he has attitudes and motives like everyone else, but they do not give his behavior its essential form. Consequently, his criminality cannot be explained satisfactorily from a psychological standpoint.

Thus, Alexander and Staub analyze criminality

into seven elemental types. It would seem, however, that not all of these types are essentially distinct. For example, the mistaken criminal, the situational criminal, and a certain type of acting-out neurotic—all bear a distinct resemblance to one another. These types fall into criminal behavior because of anti-social impulses that do not originate essentially in the personality of the individual, and all of them exhibit a more or less intact and functioning superego structure. Thus, the situational and mistaken criminals are forced to resort to criminality because events have induced certain intense emotions that threaten to engulf and destroy the integrity of their personality. Their criminal reactions, therefore, represent an attempt to regain their mental equilibrium by ridding themselves of specific noxious stimuli. Similarly, the neurotic acting-out criminal, when he uses criminality to deal with intolerable feelings of guilt, is using it as a means of restoring a composure that was destroyed by his painful guilt feelings. Thus, a fundamental criminal type, for which Alexander and Staub have discovered several different versions, resorts to criminality not as a means of expressing basic anti-social impulses but rather in an attempt to compensate for inner imbalances that have arisen in response to external forces.[9] The resulting criminal behavior may give rise to further distortions, which, in turn, may induce additional criminal activity, but the essential fact here is that crime is used to regain a lost equilibrium.

A second elemental type that Alexander and Staub have also discovered in several different forms behaves criminally because criminal behavior offers a convenient medium for expressing the basic nature of his personality. This type, which includes the organic and/or toxic criminal, the symptomatic criminal, the genuine criminal, and certain types of neurotic acting-out criminals, may or may not develop anxiety or guilt as a result of his misdeeds, but the basic source of his criminality is clearly in the personality itself. And the criminality he pursues is a direct expression of the anti-social impulses that well up within his personality.

The third basic type that Alexander and Staub describe follows a criminal path not because of any personal pathology but because he has adopted a system of values that are deviant in the larger society. The criminality of this type, which includes only the normal criminal, must be understood as an expression of his group membership; and although the psycho-dynamics of his personality may lend an idiosyncratic stamp to his behavior, its organization, in the last analysis, derives from social forces.

In all, then, Alexander and Staub seem to have identified only three elemental types: one, in which criminality helps to compensate for exogenous distortions in the individual's personality; another, in which criminality serves as a medium for the expression of basic impulses directly in action; and a third, in which criminality is sanctioned and basically defined by social groups.

Abrahamsen's Typology

A second attempt at formulating a typology of delinquency in terms of psychoanalytic theory can be found in the work of Abrahamsen, who, in the course of several essays on crime and delinquency, identifies seven distinct delinquent types. Although Abrahamsen fails to relate his types to psychoanalytic theory as closely as Alexander and Staub, he does offer some

important insights into the nature of delinquent behavior.

To begin with, Abrahamsen distinguishes between
those who are drawn into illegal behavior because of
unusual circumstances in their environment and those
whose delinquency is more immediately related to
their own psychodynamics. The first broad class he
describes as *momentary offenders* and the second as
chronic offenders.[10] And each of these general classes,
in turn, is divided into several types on the basis of
the causal factors involved.

Among the momentary offenders we find, first, the
situational delinquent, who is confronted with an
irresistible opportunity that happens incidentally to
involve him in illegal activity. He may, for example,
suddenly find himself confronted with a chance to
gain something he has wanted for some time; he may
be the victim of a gross injustice that incites him to
illegal behavior; or he may even be forced to commit a
crime in the course of defending himself from others.
But whatever the specific circumstances, his delinquency is clearly tied to the situation and is not
generally chronic. The next type, the *accidental
offender,* also finds himself involved in crime unex-
pectedly, but his misfortune arises primarily through
lapses in judgment that result in harm to others, e.g.,
the hit-and-run driver. The third type of momentary
offender, the *associational delinquent,* finds his way
into delinquency primarily because some of his friends
are inclined in that direction, and he generally displays considerable guilt and remorse about his aberration. The momentary offender, then, is swept along by
a series of events over which he has little or no
control. He reacts to his circumstances, but he does
not initiate or govern them.

The chronic offender, on the other hand, takes a more active role in his own delinquency and is not as strongly influenced by circumstances. Abrahamsen identified four types of chronic offenders. First, we have those delinquents whose criminal behavior is symptomatic of deep neurotic conflict.[11] They are driven into delinquency by some kind of irresistible compulsion, which is usually the conscious expression of unconscious sexual wishes. Included in this type, which Abrahamsen labeled the *neurotic offender,* are cleptomaniacs, pyromaniacs, and those juveniles mentioned earlier who use delinquency as a means of relieving intense unconscious guilt. The second type of chronic offender, the offender with a *character disorder,* also suffers from neurotic disturbances; but in this case, the disturbances are not incompatible with the whole structure of the individual's personality.[12] Although the neurotic offender is generally surprised and upset at his criminal actions, the offender with a character disorder usually sees little that is blameworthy in his deeds. His whole personality is involved in his behavior, and his problem is the lack of fit between his inclinations and the patterns that society expects him to follow. Included among these offenders are the psychopath, the alcoholic, the drug addict, and the homosexual. The most characteristic trait of this type is a faulty superego development that tends to leave him at the mercy of his unusual passions.

Abrahamsen's third type, *psychotic and mentally defective offenders,* includes those whose mental illness compels them to commit crimes, as for example, the schizophrenic who complies with the bizarre urgings of his "voices" or the paranoid who undertakes one day to balance the scales of "justice." It also includes those whose mental abnormality so beclouds their powers of discrimination that they are forced to take the simplest and most direct path to their goals, which incidentally involves them in delinquent behavior.[13] A fourth type that was mentioned only once by Abrahamsen consists of those offenders that have identified with a criminal way of life and who see their purposes best served through criminal behavior.[14] Such delinquents are quite incorrigible, even though they typically do not exhibit abnormal personalities. Abrahamsen gives them the unwieldy label of offenders with faulty development of the superego, but we might describe them more simply as *cultural delinquents*.

All in all, Abrahamsen breaks delinquent behavior down into seven types. Three of these are only momentarily delinquent, i.e., the situational, accidental, and the associational delinquents; three are chronically delinquent because of abnormalities in their personalities, i.e., the neurotic delinquent, the delinquent with a character disorder, and the psychotic or mentally defective delinquent; and the seventh type, the cultural delinquent, is chronically delinquent because he has allied himself with a delinquent subculture.

Abrahamsen, like Alexander and Staub earlier, draws a clear distinction between the neurotic delinquent who cannot keep himself from committing crimes and the delinquent with a character disorder whose problem essentially stems from an incongruence between his native responses and conventional folkways. Abrahamsen's main interest, however, is not theoretical; and unfortunately, he has afforded little attention to the psychodynamic forces that are responsible for each of these patterns.

Friedlander's Typology of Delinquency

Friedlander, another student of psychoanalysis, has also attempted to categorize delinquents in terms of their psychodynamic properties; but unlike our first two theorists, she has done so in terms of three basic complexes that form, she suggests, the basis of most delinquent behavior. The source of much, if not most delinquency, according to Friedlander, is an *anti-social character formation* in which the juvenile is prevented from adjusting adequately to his social environment by serious defects in his psychological capacities.[15] More specifically, such a person is often so impetuous and egocentric that his behavior tends to be controlled largely by the needs of the moment and the opportunities of the situation. Because of his marriage to the concrete and the immediate, the juvenile eventually finds it difficult to negotiate those situations that require a systematic, organized adjustment to the future as well as to the present. Ultimately, as he grows older and his responsibilities multiply, the juvenile's deficiencies become painfully apparent; and his alienation from his parents, teachers, and neighbors grows to irremedial proportions. Resentment and revenge are added to his other character deficiencies and his delinquency emerges in full bloom. Such juveniles become anti-social, therefore, because their character structure does not allow them to fulfill the routine demands society makes on them as they mature into adolescence.

Their character structure remains immature primarily because of serious imbalances in their psychological development.[16] Their instinctive urges, for example, still bear an infantile stamp in that they focus principally upon basic needs and tend to be massive in their proportions. Partly as a result of their powerful instinctual needs, their ego-development has never progressed beyond the pleasure principle, and the ego has never really established itself as master of the id. Such individuals are often skillful in gaining their momentary desires from the environment—their egos can exploit the present situation effectively—but they are rarely able to deny altogether or even postpone the importunings of the id. Moreover, their superegos have typically failed to develop to the point where they can control and inhibit immoral behavior. Such boys generally have only a loose identification with their fathers and, accordingly, have failed to develop the self-control of the more conventional person. Hence, they feel little disinclination to commit illegal acts when left unsupervised. All in all, then, the strength of their instinctive needs, the infantile nature of their superegos, and the weakness of their egos serve to orient these juveniles rather narrowly to egocentric needs and compel them to violate the basic prohibitions of society.

Juveniles unfortunate enough to possess such character structures generally exhibit anti-social behavior at the onset of latency, i.e., at the age of five or six, when other children are beginning to lose some of their infantile mannerisms. The intensity of their difficulties, however, continues to mount until, soon after puberty, their delinquency becomes habitual, and the likelihood of the youngsters' becoming common offenders in adulthood is great. Their delinquent behavior needs no provocation, and it generally continues in spite of any adjustments that are made in the environment. It is inherent in their character structure.

A second factor that is also relevant to delinquency

from Friedlander's viewpoint is the degree of neurotic involvement found in the personality of the offender. While a neurotic disturbance in itself will not usually provoke an anti-social response, if it occurs in conjunction with an anti-social character formation, it will tend to orient and color the nature of the delinquency that does arise.

Neurotic disturbances take many forms and the blending of neurotic tendencies with an anti-social character structure can produce many different types of delinquent behavior. The essential fact that identifies all neurotic delinquents, however, is the symbolic nature of their delinquency.[17] In every case, their delinquency represents some other action that the juvenile unconsciously desires to express—often against a parent or sibling—but does not dare to do so because of its hideous nature. Instead, a delinquent act that is analogous to the repressed wish is performed against someone else. Typical forms of such neurotic delinquency include cleptomania in which stealing does not directly arise as a result of pronounced character defects but rather out of lapses in the superego and ego that make it possible for unconscious desires of a sexual or aggressive nature occasionally to break through into consciousness in symbolic form. The actual content of the neurotic symptom depends, of course, upon the specific nature of the individual's unconscious and his previous history; but not infrequently, according to Friedlander, it takes the form of stealing.[18]

The third general factor behind delinquent behavior consists of disturbances in the physiology of the juvenile such that his ego-processes are seriously damaged.[19] Such individuals, like those with an anti-social character formation, find it difficult to conform to the routines of conventional society; but in this case, the difficulty arises as a result of organic defects of one sort or another.

These, then, are the three basic complexes, or factors, according to Friedlander, that are behind most delinquency. But since many delinquents exhibit more than one condition in their make-up, the typology that emerges on the basis of these factors is rather complex.[20]

In addition to the juvenile whose delinquency is primarily an outgrowth of an anti-social character structure, Friedlander describes three types with varying degrees of anti-social character formation and varying types of neurotic tendency. There is, first, the juvenile whose anti-social character is not quite as pronounced as in the pure type. Typically, his delinquency commences later, i.e., during puberty instead of latency, and is triggered by an environmental pressure or crisis. The second type also exhibits an anti-social character structure to only a moderate degree, but, in addition, he suffers from serious neurotic conflicts that induce symptom formation. In the absence of an anti-social character, such conflicts would merely give rise to a neurosis; but because of the anti-social orientation of the character structure, the symptoms tend to take a delinquent direction. Many sexual offenses are of this type, as are also cleptomania, incendiarism, and many so-called spontaneous, irrational offenses.

A third type also exhibits an anti-social character structure with neurotic tendencies, but in this case the delinquent behavior is not so much the symptom of a repressed wish as it is the embodiment of a more or less conscious libidinal desire.[21] Thus, the lying and stealing of the passive psychopathic personality is sometimes based on the sexual connotation that a dialogue of accusation and denial holds for the offender. The essential difference between this type and the second lies in the fact that in this case, the neurotic conflict leads to the direct acting-out of psychic needs, whereas in the preceding type the neurotic conflict gives rise to only symptomatic behavior.

In this fashion, Friedlander describes four types of delinquents in terms of their psychological characteristics. She also distinguishes four additional types on the basis of their organic or psychotic pathologies. The only common thread running through these last four types, however, is the damage suffered by the individual's ego-processes at the hands of the pathology.[22] In the first place, we have those juveniles whose adaptive abilities are crippled by toxic substances, e.g., drugs or alcoholic beverages. Second, we have those whose smooth adjustment to society is impeded by organic pathologies, like mental defectiveness, tumors, or encephalitis. Third, we have those individuals whose egos are impaired because of diseases of the central nervous system, e.g., epilepsy or cerebral dysrhythmia. And finally, there are those whose delinquency derives from psychotic impairment in which the difference between wish and reality is not maintained.

It is clear that we have in Friedlander's analysis only four elemental delinquent patterns. First, she describes the delinquent whose primitive urges and lack of self-control make it increasingly difficult for him to find a place in conventional groups. Since these delinquents are oriented almost exclusively to the immediate environment, their impulsive, undisciplined crimes will be tied for the most part to the opportunities of their immediate vicinity. The second type presents essentially the same character defects that plague the first, but, in addition, he suffers from neurotic conflicts that incline his delinquent behavior along distinctive lines. Instead of the erratic, explosive pattern that is characteristic of the first type, this type will tend to fall into a criminal pattern that expresses symbolically his underlying conflicts. Thus, he will focus upon crimes that are of a sexual and/or destructive nature; and although his crimes will be just as compulsive as with the first type, they will not have the same aimless, wanton quality.

A question might be raised, however, as to whether neurotic conflicts can arise among delinquents who also exhibit an anti-social character structure. Does not the absence of a well developed superego prevent an individual from repressing tabooed impulses, and, indeed, is not the inability to repress these impulses one reason why individuals with an anti-social character structure find it so difficult to gain acceptance in conventional society? Friedlander implies that the dominant factor in the behavior of this type of individual is the neurotic conflict and that the weaknesses accompanying the anti-social character formation are still largely incipient. Thus, the individual's superego is sufficiently intact to enable him to repress socially condemned impulses and develop unconscious conflicts, while at the same time his control processes are sufficiently damaged to permit the expression of his unconscious conflicts in the form of anti-social behavior instead of neurotic symptoms. Those with a well developed anti-social character formation, however, probably could not suffer from troublesome conflicts because of their weak, infantile superegos.

Friedlander's third type resembles the second in that it, too, combines an anti-social character formation with neurotic needs. In this case, however, the neu-rotic problem does not center upon a conflict, but rather upon an inability to sublimate. The psycho-sexual development of such individuals has advanced to the point where their libidinal desires can narrow down to specific objects, but the control functions in the personality have not developed to the point where forbidden desires *can be* successfully repressed. Thus, we have an individual who is midway between the normal personality structure and the anti-social char-acter structure in which the unconscious and the conscious are more or less fused.

It might help to understand these three patterns more clearly if they are conceived of as arranged along a continuum in which the normal, integrated per-sonality is gradually dismantled, function by function, until at the extreme pole we have the primitive, uncomplicated anti-social character structure. At the one pole, then, we have a normal personality that permits the individual a good adjustment to his en-vironment because the conscience, while keeping un-acceptable impulses in check in the unconscious, remains sufficiently relaxed to allow for their sublima-tion in certain forms of behavior. Moreover, in the normal personality the ego is sufficiently strong to gain satisfaction directly or indirectly for most of the individual's needs through commerce with the en-vironment. The normal personality, therefore, is not so diffuse and unstructured as to become obnoxious to the community, but neither is it so impermeable vis-à-vis the unconscious that the individual is colorless and unimaginative.

The next position on the continuum is occupied by the delinquent who has an incipient anti-social char-acter formation but whose psychic structure is still sufficiently intact so that troublesome neurotic conflicts may develop within the unconscious. In the third position, we have the delinquent whose personality has been damaged to the point that he is unable to control himself effectively but whose motive structure has developed enough to allow some discrimination in relating to his environment. And finally, at the other extreme, we have the delinquent with an anti-social character formation who has neither a neurotic conflict nor a refined motive structure. He cannot adjust to society because it demands more in the way of self-control and discrimination than he possesses.

The fourth psychological type defined by Friedlander, the delinquent with organic impairments, corresponds to none of these first three types because its psychodynamics are much simpler. Delinquency here can be thought of as the result of an ego collapse in an otherwise reasonably socialized personality. Considerable moral anxiety is usually generated in such cases and turbulent unconscious needs may also induce some neurotic anxiety, but the individual's behavior is dominated essentially by the need to regain composure. If drugs are his solution, his delinquency will proceed along one path. If a paranoid transformation is his solution, his delinquency will unfold along a different path. But whatever solution is dominant, delinquency in this type is incidental to the more pressing problem of regaining self-control, and the pattern of delinquency that emerges will be determined by the means selected to regain control. This type is essentially different from the first three types however, and for this reason may not be logically fitted in the continuum just described.

Sanford's Typology of Inmates

Sanford is a fourth theorist who has sought to define a typology of deviant behavior in terms of psychoanalytic theory. But in this case, we are dealing with a typology of adult criminals, not delinquents, developed by a social psychologist, not a practicing psychiatrist. Sanford has had considerable experience with adult, male convicts, and in an early article he attempted to analyze some of the types he has encountered.[23] Although he was concerned exclusively with adults, his types are also identifiable among juveniles and for this reason are appropriate for consideration here.

According to Sanford, the *presocial criminal* is characterized by an infantile superego and an ego that is weak and unable to cope with the primitive demands of the id. His crimes are not so vicious as they are annoying and chronic. He has weak but conventional guilt feelings, but since the superego is of little help in curbing the id, the id usually prevails. He is often a model prisoner, adapting readily both to the authoritarianism of the institution and to the inmate culture. He is essentially a weak character, not vicious, but easily swayed by more forceful types.

The *anti-social criminal*, on the other hand, has a severe superego and a strong ego. His criminality seems to stem basically from a deep desire to repudiate and subvert the larger society. In the process of defying society, however, the sanctions of his superego inevitably become increasingly censorious, and he is ultimately forced into a full identification with the underworld. He is intensely loyal to his compatriots and the code of the underworld, and in prison he is regarded as a "right guy." He is unflagging in his resistance to prison authorities, but with fellow inmates he is sympathetic and cooperative within the framework of the inmate code. With this type, the id is under firm control and the ego is effective. The superego, however, is insulated from the rest of the personality, and there is considerable unconscious guilt. To compensate for this guilt, the individual must receive not only constant reassurance from his compatriots that he is moral in terms of the criminal code but also periodic punishment from the authorities.

Sanford's third type stands in sharp contrast to these first two. The *asocial criminal* combines a weak, almost inoperative superego together with an ego that is strong and equal to its task. The libido is attached to the ego and as a result we have a criminal who is egocentric and narcissistic. The absence of any systematic superego controls means further that he is capable of almost anything, and the strength of his ego means that he will be particularly effective in carrying out his selfish purposes. He is exploitative and amoral, turning every situation to his advantage regardless of the consequences. In prison he is a problem to the other inmates as well as the authorities.

In formulating this typology, Sanford lays no claim to exhausting the range of types implied by psychoanalytic theory—indeed, he mentions a fourth type, the impulsive-addictive criminal, which, he suggests, has been described in full detail by others. But he does identify three types that are readily distinguishable in delinquent populations, and for this reason his observations have been examined here.

Weinberg's Typology of Delinquency

The last typology that we shall discuss is distinctive in several respects. First of all, it is the only typology of delinquency we shall examine that does not make extensive use of the psychoanalytic framework in defining its types. Weinberg does not reject psychoanalytic theory, but he does not describe his types explicitly in terms of that point of view. Second, the typology represents a summary of the insights and conclusions of others more than it does an original typology drawn from any particular body of theory. And finally, it depends heavily upon a theory of socialization to explain the nature of the types that make up the typology.

Weinberg's typology is instructive on several counts. It is thoroughly documented, and its types are fully and carefully described. But it also illustrates the dangers that inhere in any attempt to define a psychological typology of delinquency without a theory of personality clearly in mind. Because he fails to make consistent use of a formal theory of personality, Weinberg tends to neglect the intervening role that personality plays between behavior and environmental pressures. In explaining the behavior of his delinquent types, he often falls back upon an analysis of their environmental conditions instead of an analysis of their psychological structure. Thus, the psychopath is a deprived child who was ignored largely as an infant; not a juvenile, for example, whose libido is stunted and primitive, incapable of supporting the emotions of love or gratitude. But the first task the typologist must face is that of defining the psychodynamics *underlying* the behavior of the types that are identified. *Only* after this objective has been gained can he turn his attention to the social conditions that tend to produce these particular types. The sociologist who rejects, either explicitly or implicitly, the validity of a psychological theory of personality may be tempted to explain behavior directly in terms of socialization experiences. In so doing, however, he unwisely assumes that the relationship between environment and behavior, which is in reality distant and rather indirect, is close and immediate.

Weinberg's typology itself is based upon four types: the "true" psychopath; the acting-out neurotic; the self-centered, overindulged person; and the cultural deviant. In approaching these four types, we shall focus primarily upon his descriptions of their characteristics, for the most part ignoring the reasons Weinberg gives for their becoming what they are.

The *"true" psychopath,* according to Weinberg, presents a distinctive set of characteristics.[24] He lacks, for example, the ability to postpone the satisfaction of each urge as it comes upon him, and he has little capacity for remorse or guilt. Although he can relate adequately on an impersonal, casual level; he is rarely able to sustain intimate relationships, because his emotional responses to others are very limited. He is, in short, egocentric, irresponsible in the extreme, and emotionally shallow.

The psychology of the psychopath is dominated by several facts.[25] First, as a result of an emotionally barren environment in infancy, the psychopath's emotional development never progresses beyond the infantile level; and his emotions in maturity remain shallow, simple, and direct. The absence of strong attachments during childhood, moreover, means that the psychopath is relatively inured against withdrawal of affection as a method of control and that there are few internalized ideals to guide and sanction his conduct in the absence of direct supervision. The psychopath, therefore, is deprived of a sense of direction in the form of moral prohibitions or refined intuitions and by default must preoccupy himself with the immediate and the concrete.

The *acting-out neurotic* presents quite a different picture.[26] For example, he can form attachments with others, and he does have a conscience. Indeed, one of his problems is the hostility that wells up within him as a defense against deep feelings of guilt. But his alienation from those he loves tends to increase his unconscious guilt, which, in turn, aggravates his hostility and ultimately his isolation. Thus, he seems to be in a vicious circle: his reaction to his situation makes his situation even more distressing. Like the psychopath, then, he seems to move from one difficulty to the next, essentially wedded to the moment and helpless to alter his maladaptive behavior.

The *self-centered, overindulged person* according to Weinberg also bears a certain superficial resemblance to the psychopath. For example, he rarely experiences intense guilt from his misdeeds; he suffers little from free-floating anxiety; and he is inclined to exploit others to his own advantage. But he usually does have a close relationship with at least one parent—and he certainly cannot be accused of being emotionally shallow. This delinquent is so overindulged as a child that the usual relationship between child and parent is reversed, and in effect he comes to dominate his parents. He exhibits wide emotional swings in which a flirtatious charm alternates with intemperate, aggressive outbursts.[27]

The *cultural deviant* differs from the aforementioned types in that he is delinquent primarily because he was enculturated in a value-system that is considered deviant by the larger society. To all intents and purposes, he is a perfectly normal member of a deviant subculture and usually displays the psychological patterns that are customarily found in members of his community. When judged by standards other than his own, however, such delinquents may appear psychologically deviant, and they may even be diagnosed as psychopathic.[28]

This, then, is Weinberg's psychological typology of delinquency. He has given a minimum attention to the inner dynamics of each type, while taking great care to describe the socializing experiences that give rise to the types in the first place. We have here, however, confined our remarks primarily to the characteristics of each type.

In classifying the delinquents in this fashion, Weinberg has not pretended to exhaust the full range of delinquent types. The objective of his analysis was to distinguish several delinquent types that have often been incorrectly described as psychopathic. He does not repudiate the validity of the psychopath as a distinctive type, but he is concerned that other delinquent types that present some of the psychopath's characteristics not be mistakenly classified as psychopathic. As a result, Weinberg has self-consciously limited his attention to a narrow range of the delinquent spectrum.

Each of the typologies we have examined here represents an attempt to identify the attitudinal and motivational sources of delinquent behavior. Although there is considerable agreement among these typologies, at least two different approaches to the problem of delinquency are discernible. Thus, Alex-

ander and Staub, Abrahamsen, and Sanford use the
ego, superego, and id as their basic concepts and
derive their types from the manner in which these
psychological constructs can theoretically interrelate.
Friedlander, on the other hand, examines the psychodynamic complexes that seem to underlie delinquent
behavior; and after describing these in detail, she
suggests that several delinquent types can be derived
by combining these elemental complexes. The latter
strategy, of course, permits greater flexibility in interpreting individual cases, but it does not yield any
greater number of types, since there can only be one
type for each basic complex. Combining different
complexes does not yield genotypes but simply hybrids.

Although none of these authors has self-consciously
constructed an ideal typology of delinquent behavior, their considerable agreement suggests that psychological theory is sufficiently well developed to yield an
exhaustive typology of delinquency. And accordingly,
I shall conclude this chapter by proposing a typology
of delinquency phrased in terms of psychoanalytic
theory. All the types I shall describe were mentioned
by one or more of the five theorists examined in this
chapter, and several have been described by them in
close detail.

On the basis of what we have already seen, it should
be apparent that there are three distinct ways in
which psychological processes contribute directly to
delinquent behavior. First, we have those delinquents
whose anti-social orientation is rooted in the very core
of their personalities. Such adolescents become delinquent because their own immanent impulses throw
them into direct conflict with the mores of their
society. There are, of course, several different ways in

which the adolescent's personality can compel him to violate the laws and mores of his community and each of these is the basis for a distinctive type, but the thread tying them all together is the fact that the individual's "normal" personality is inconsistent with the normative patterns of his community.

A second process that also tends to induce delinquent behavior is that in which the adolescent's personality is dominated by internal stress to such an extent that he finds it impossible to conform to the intricate and demanding patterns of his community. Such individuals do not turn to delinquency as a convenient means of expressing their basic inclinations; instead, they do so as a reaction to exceptional and disorienting guilt and anxieties. But their personalities are not basically anti-social, since they only resort to this mode of behavior as a response to their inner turmoil.

A third way in which psychological forces also contribute to delinquency is via the unconscious. When certain basic needs are denied a minimal degree of gratification in conscious behavior, the energy behind these repressed needs grows until the personality is obliged to acknowledge their presence in symbolic form. The basic needs themselves are not directly gratified, since the conscious part of the mind cannot admit their existence. But they are so insistent in the unconscious that some kind of psychosomatic adjustment to their demands is forced on the personality. The symptoms that arise represent a compromise between the revulsion felt by the mind for these needs and the insistent demand that they be expressed and gratified in some way. Not every symptom that emerges in this fashion oversteps the limits of society, but those that do essentially represent the reaction of the personality to forces that are not integral to its organization. Hence, the resulting delinquent behavior cannot be described as a *direct* expression of the individual's deepest motives, but neither is it a desperate reaction to stress and inner turmoil. Thus, unconscious pressures can give rise to a distinctive pattern of delinquent behavior and must be considered apart from the rest.

There are then, three distinct psychological processes that contribute to the delinquency of adolescents, each of which corresponds to a general class of delinquents: *the impulsive delinquent,* who becomes delinquent because the basic direction of his personality happens to be anti-social; *the neurotic delinquent,* whose delinquency stems from the fact that the normal expression of his personality is thwarted by a disorganizing anxiety; and *the symptomatic delinquent,* who is compelled to violate the laws and mores of his society by the pressures of his unconscious. It is within these three broad classes that I intend to locate several specific delinquent types.

Impulsive Delinquency

Impulsive delinquents can be differentiated from one another by four criteria. First, they can be distinguished in terms of the aims of their dominant motives, i.e., whether they are oriented to conventional or unconventional values and ideals. Second, they can be differentiated by the degree to which their dominant motives are refined and discriminating, or insensitive to the various alternatives in the environment. Third, they can be distinguished from one another by the intensity of their dominant motives and, finally, by their ability to inhibit or control these dominant motives. Using these criteria we can identify four different types within this class: the unsocialized aggressive child; the self-centered indulged child; the psychopath; and the sexual pervert.

The Unsocialized Aggressive Child

The unsocialized aggressive child probably comes as close to being a primitive, animal-like personality as a human being can. His emotions are elemental and vicious. He rarely expresses any feelings but anger, frustration, rage, or hostility, and these are often massive and poorly resolved. Moreover, his emotions are indiscriminate, since he rarely exhibits any preferences or inhibitions regarding the objects of his emotions. He can be as violent toward an inoffensive child as an insulting, belligerent peer. Thus, because his emotions are unrefined, he may choose inappropriate objects for the satisfaction of his basic impulses. His motive structure is not perverse, however, it is just that his emotions are massive and undiscriminating.

The ego controls of this type, moreover, are virtually nonexistent. He may give the impression of being a strong personality because of his combativeness, but he is helpless before the onslaught of his emotions and useless in intricate or long-range projects of any complexity. He does not, in other words, possess a strong or effective ego. And, finally, his superego structure is practically inoperative. He may be responsive to shame and ridicule—perhaps because of a low self-esteem—but he does not exhibit remorse, guilt, or discouragement for his past or future. Indeed, he is remarkable for his carefree gaiety in the face of disaster and defeat, and he is as little mindful of his own welfare as he is of others'. Thus, in terms of the criteria outlined above, his emotions are distinctive for their intensity, their almost exclusively aggressive tone, and their lack of discrimination. The dominant motives are not so perverse as random, and control of either a positive or a negative sort is largely absent. He has neither the capacity to inhibit his more urgent motives nor the ability to guide them. He is, in short, unsocialized.

With all of these limitations, his behavior could not help but be explosively aggressive; random and disorganized; and at least periodically anti-social. It is doubtful, in fact, that he could adjust adequately to any kind of organized social life at all. His delinquent behavior should appear early—at about the point when his peers are beginning to move into the more demanding and complicated levels in elementary schools—and it should be little influenced by any of the usual remedial efforts.

Several of the authors mentioned above have commented upon this type. To Alexander and Staub he was the genuine criminal; and Friedlander would undoubtedly regard him as suffering from an anti-social character formation. Although Abrahamsen described a general category that corresponds to the anti-social delinquent, namely, the offender with a character disorder, he fails to narrow this description down in terms corresponding closely to the unsocialized aggressive child.

Thanks to Hewitt and Jenkins we have a rather complete account of the genesis of this type.[29] The family is often profoundly disorganized in that even when it is intact there is very little solidarity. The mother, in particular, is frequently disturbed and/or anti-social in her own behavior, although her own tendencies in this regard are not the *primary* factor in the child's delinquency. Rather, her pathology seems to prevent her from adequately fulfilling the responsibilities of motherhood, and as a result, the child is typically subjected to a general and unrelenting rejection throughout infancy and early childhood. Such a profound rejection, of course, could not help but have drastic effects upon the child's capacity for love, gratitude, sympathy, and self-control. Due to the deeply pathological character of this early experience, then, aggressive feelings and a callous disregard for the welfare of others come to dominate his orientation to the world, and a pervasive sense of personal futility and worthlessness dominate his feelings toward himself. Unfortunately, there is very little that society can do to lift his burden.

The Self-Centered Indulged Delinquent

The self-centered indulged delinquent, like the unsocialized aggressive child, has been carefully studied by a number of authors. In addition to Weinberg, who describes him as the self-centered, overindulged person, Sanford regards him as an asocial criminal; Mahler as an *enfant terrible;* Levy as an overprotected child; and the Gluecks as an endomorphic delinquent.[30]

There is close agreement among these writers regarding the behavior of this type. He conforms rather closely to the Dr. Jekyl–Mr. Hyde syndrome, in that he seems to combine a facile, congenial manner with an egocentric, salacious temperament. When he is the center of attention and his plans are proceeding smoothly, he can display a rare charm and graciousness; but when he is faced with a threat to his position or objective, he shifts to an intense anger that can very quickly mount to dangerous, vicious proportions.

It cannot be said, however, that he is unsocialized. He can, for example, feel positive emotions like tenderness and sympathy, particularly for women, and he does emotionally discriminate in the usual ways. He feels sexual impulses only toward the opposite sex, and his aggressive feelings are usually reserved for the same sex. His dominant motives, therefore, are oriented along conventional lines, and they are sufficiently refined to make most of the normal distinctions between appropriate and inappropriate objects.

His acting-out characteristics seem to be based upon an extremely intense and volatile emotional structure and an unusually weak capacity to inhibit or divert his more destructive impulses. When faced with delay, resistance, or opposition, his immediate response is one of annihilation; and in the heat of anger, his whole being is devoted to this goal. Unlike more conventional individuals, he does not usually experience pity or empathy for his victims; and, consequently, he will press his attack far beyond the point that is necessary simply to discourage an opponent. He is, therefore, potentially dangerous to those who might stand in his way. In contrast to the unsocialized aggressive child, however, his lack of self-control is not complete. Although he is unable to *suppress* his more powerful impulses, he can focus and organize their expression along purposeful lines.[31]

Socially, this child might manage a moderately successful adjustment insofar as he is not subjected to entangling restraints fairly late in childhood. But if adolescence brings with it additional duties and more intricate responsibilities, his impatience at such restrictions will quickly become pronounced, and his anti-social activity will mount accordingly. Thus, shortly after puberty his impulsivity should begin to be a problem to the community.

The forces that are responsible for the development

of the self-centered indulged delinquent center primarily in the family. Although the family is typically quite stable and accepted in the community, it does present an unusual structural imbalance. The mother is pre-eminently the powerful figure, and the father plays only a marginal and insignificant role vis-à-vis the other members. The mother and the children—particularly the male children—are the center of the family, and the father is a tolerated but unwelcomed intruder. According to Mahler, this child is the product of an overly attentive mother who subtly excites the boy's Oedipal desires, while the impotent father is unable to force the boy to relinquish these impulses in favor of a thoroughgoing paternal identification.[32] Thus, the child's passions and emotions are continually at a high pitch, whereas his inability finally to identify with his father deprives him of the ability to exercise self-restraint and control. Thus, instead of resolving the Oedipus complex in the usual manner with a firm masculine identification, he remains at the phallic stage, emotionally responsive to his mother but hostile and rejecting toward his father. In adolescence he continues the pattern, but, unfortunately, some of his emotional impulsivity generally becomes sufficiently anti-social to create a great deal of trouble for himself and the community.

The Psychopath

These first two types of delinquents combine a volatile impulsivity, a capacity for intense violence, and an inability to exercise effective restraints in such a way that their chances of escaping an anti-social career are very slim, indeed. In contrast, however, the "true" psychopath, as Weinberg calls him, suffers only from an inability to inhibit his more exploitative desires in deference either to the well-being of his close associates or to the requirements of communal living. He is immune to the entreaties or reproaches of others, but at the same time he is unable himself to channel his behavior to his own long-range advantage.

He does not exhibit, however, the same readiness to burst into violence that the unsocialized aggressive child does, nor does he display the same volatility that the self-centered indulged delinquent does. Moreover, although his motivational patterns may be oriented to rather tangible and immediate purposes, he does seek conventional values, and he does make many of the appropriate discriminations in selecting partners for gratifying his sexual needs. In other words, the aim of his dominant motives is more or less conventional; and although his ability to distinguish among appropriate and inappropriate objects is limited, it is not entirely absent.

Nor is he unpredictably violent or abusive. He will resist bullying by others, but his first response to frustration or resistance is not aggression but circumvention. His problem, therefore, centers upon an emotional callousness that foils the attempts of others to influence or control his behavior. He is enabled thereby to wend his way through life unmindful of the inconvenience or pain that his irresponsibility may cause others. Inevitably, however, in the course of his wanderings, he commits a number of anti-social acts that are more notable for their irritant value than for their vicious or destructive quality.

The development of the psychopath, though still debated, is rather well understood. Fenichel suggests, as does Weinberg, that the absence of stable attachments with adults in the first years of life render the child unable to experience the usual kinds of positive, tender emotions for others.[33] Although we might expect such basic deprivations to arouse considerable frustration and an inclination to act out aggression, such apparently is not the case. The barren nature of the early environment, seems to leave the child incapable of intense emotion of any kind and, thus, emotionally remote from others.

The Sexual Pervert

The last example of impulsive delinquency, the homosexual, is probably the least violent but the most despised of all. His whole problem, of course, is based upon his sexual feelings for members of the same sex. Nevertheless, his discrimination among sexual objects is usually quite refined—he is attracted to certain individuals and not others; and the intensity of his homosexual desire is not generally overwhelming, although it may be persistent. And, finally, he is not ordinarily prone to other kinds of delinquent behavior, i.e., he is not unduly exploitative or aggressive in nonsexual matters. In short, although the aim of his sexual motives is perverse, aside from his sexual aberration, his motivational structure is usually discriminating and oriented along conventional lines. Moreover, he does not seem to suffer from a primitive or inoperative superego. He often does feel guilt at some level about his abnormality, and he is emotionally responsive to the attitudes of others. His inner restraints, however, are not sufficient to inhibit the perversion altogether; and although he may be ambivalent about it, he usually yields to the desire to act out his unconventional sexual impulses.

The genesis of the male homosexual is only incompletely understood, but according to Fenichel, it stems from an identification with the mother instead of the father and a consequent assumption of a feminine orientation toward males.[34] The identification with the mother can be precipitated by a number of factors —a viewing of the mother's genitals or a deep fear of his own aggressiveness—but the result is the same, a fear or disgust for females as sexual objects. The nature of the homosexuality, i.e., whether it assumes an active or passive form, depends largely upon the individual's psychosexual experience prior to his fateful identification with the mother. The active homosexual, for example, is likely to be an individual who managed a phallic adjustment before he identified with his mother and who was motivated to seek young passive males as sexual objects because their similarity to his own nature at the time of his identification with his mother provides an outlet for his phallic narcissism. The passive homosexual, on the other hand, is dominated by an anal fixation and a desire to incorporate the male genital in the same manner as the mother. Thus, there are several forms of homosexuality—all of which represent a type of impulsive behavior that is delinquent.

We have in this discussion examined four distinct types of delinquents, each of which presents an easily recognizable pattern of characteristics. They all, however, are similar with regard to at least one quality: all incline in a delinquent direction because the basic orientation of their dominant motives leads to behavior that is intolerable to the community.

Neurotic Delinquency

The neurotic delinquent, as we have already indicated, becomes delinquent in an attempt to correct an imbalance or distortion in the inner dynamics of his personality. Thus, his delinquency does not spring directly from the depths of his personality; instead, it is often an incidental result of the individual's attempts to restore an original equilibrium that was lost.

The Inadequate Delinquent

The best example of the neurotic delinquent is the delinquent with an inadequate personality or, more simply, the inadequate delinquent. In contrast to the impulsive delinquent, the inadequate delinquent has been socialized in a reasonably normal fashion and if left to himself would not usually feel compelled to violate the mores of the community. His motives are ordinarily oriented toward conventional objects; he usually makes most of the appropriate discriminations among these objects; and his basic anti-social impulses are not originally so intense that they cannot be controlled most of the time. His difficulty stems from an inability to compose himself sufficiently to allow a minimally acceptable adjustment within an increasingly complex and demanding social environment. In short, his ego is not sufficient to the social tasks he is expected to fulfill; and eventually, his ego, in effect, goes on strike.[35]

The collapse of the ego, however, raises a host of additional problems for the adolescent to bear. First, he often finds that he is helpless before the demands of his more pressing needs, and as a result, he is relentlessly pushed hither and yon in a frantic search for outlets or satisfactions for his drives. Inevitably, his orientation shifts to the concrete and immediate and leaves him incapable of carrying forward any but the simplest and most momentary of projects. His general incompetence, however, simply adds to his alienation from conventional friends, parents, and teachers and increases his sense of disgrace. Deep feelings of inadequacy and despair come to dominate his attitudes about himself and further dull any desire to grapple constructively with his problems. All in all, as his ego controls give way, the inadequate delinquent becomes more conscious of his immediate needs, less mindful of any long-range requirements he may ultimately face, and deeply overwhelmed with guilt. In effect, he is immobilized as far as any purposeful, constructive activity is concerned.

His disgrace and alienation, then, foreshadow his delinquency and indirectly cause it. The initial deterioration in ego controls is often preceded by a rather lengthy experience of humiliation and denigration, which typically produces a powerful, unconscious desire for vengeance and counteraggression. The desire to revenge himself upon his tormentors, however, provokes considerable guilt, since his conscience cannot acknowledge vicious, destructive impulses without acting to curb them. Moreover, the guilt and despair that grip the boy tend also to weaken his ego controls even further by destroying his hope that action in the present can have a beneficial influence upon his future. Thus, he is bitter and resentful; he is engulfed with feelings of guilt and worthlessness; and he is unable to mobilize these troublesome feelings toward constructive ends. It is almost inevitable that some of his hatred should spill over into overt anti-social activity.

The depredations of the inadequate delinquent, however, are almost never directed at his original tormentors or at least not in a straightforward manner that would confront them face-to-face. His early humiliations and his weakened ego structure generally incline him to more devious and less hazardous forms of aggression, e.g., vandalism or theft. The ultimate result of his venting his resentment, however, is simply further disgrace, deeper despair, and more overwhelming guilt. Thus, if delinquency is utilized at first as a means of relieving some of his anxieties and aggressive needs, it serves only to create even more serious anxieties and more powerful feelings of revenge and resentment.

In one guise or another the inadequate delinquent has been studied and commented upon by a large number of authors. It can be readily seen that Alexander and Staub regard him as a neurotic acting-out criminal; that Abrahamsen describes him along with some other types as the neurotic delinquent; that Sanford describes him as a presocial criminal; and that Weinberg sees him as the acting-out neurotic.[36]

According to the picture presented by these authors, this child is usually the product of a home in which hostility is an ever-present factor and parental inconsistencies both in what is actually done and in what is done and said is the prevailing pattern. Thus, there is little chance for the child to develop a firm sense of security; and when confronted with difficult trials in the community, he has little strength with which to master them. It is undoubtedly true, moreover, that those groups in our society that are systematically exposed to humiliation and denigration, e.g., lower-class Negroes or working-class boys in middle-class high schools, are most susceptible to this kind of reaction pattern.

The Crystallized Delinquent

The crystallized delinquent and the inadequate delinquent have a great deal in common. The delinquency of each represents a neurotic reaction to the press of disturbing and alien emotions in the personality. The inadequate delinquent is forced into delinquency because his anxiety and fears are so overwhelming that he cannot tame his primitive impulses and effectively discharge his responsibilities. His delinquency, therefore, results from an inability to contain himself. The crystallized delinquent, however, becomes delinquent for a more direct reason. For him, delinquency represents a way of containing himself and of *mastering* his inner turmoil.

The crystallized delinquent has been only incompletely studied, but in terms of what is known at this point, it would appear that the psychodynamics of the crystallized delinquent are as follows.[37] His basic personality is not anti-social in that he entertains the usual interests and restraints in his relations with others. His feelings toward the opposite sex, for example, are conventional and controllable, while his destructive impulses are not explosive or unpredictable. In short, his basic needs are not, initially at least, inconsistent with the conventional demands of society. Moreover, his ego and superego are intact and functioning in reasonably effective ways, too. His delinquency does not stem, in other words, from overly intense drives or weak inner controls.

The problem for which delinquency is such a convenient solution is the presence in his unconscious of a deep and pervasive sense of guilt. This guilt, of course, can arise in any number of ways, but if it is not satisfactorily resolved, it presents the individual with an unusual problem. In the first place, it damages his self-esteem and undermines his desire to take his place in conventional society.[38] His feelings of guilt and inadequacy will not allow him to pretend that he is superior in any regard. Furthermore, he often feels quite strongly that those who do belong to conventional groups are engaged in what amounts to a hollow sham. Not only is he inadequate, but so is everyone else, even those who are generally acknowledged as being virtuous and superior. His sense of guilt and the accompanying feelings of inadequacy, therefore, prevent his entering most kinds of conventional groups and lead to a cynicism regarding the motives of those who do.

His unconscious guilt and sense of inferiority also tend to increase his experiences of conflict with others. Although he may acknowledge his own shortcomings, he cannot tolerate others who also point them out. Thus, criticisms and condemnations tend to arouse a strong desire to eliminate their authors and should his critics persist, he will generally take steps to silence them. These crystallized delinquents sense that they cannot safely accommodate much more guilt and self-doubt, and they will accordingly try to demolish those who insist upon criticizing them. In the course of their attempts to establish an inner composure, then, such individuals find themselves increasingly drawn into combative relationships.

It is apparent why delinquency offers an inviting solution to the interpersonal difficulties of such persons. First, it is sufficiently illegitimate to enable the adolescent to avoid pretentious claims of virtue and self-worth. In becoming delinquent, he need not claim that he is morally superior to anyone. Second, it serves to institutionalize his conflicts with his detractors and sanction his desires to revenge himself upon them. And, finally, it serves to relieve some of his guilt, since in being apprehended and punished he atones periodically for his unconscious sense of being evil. Once his debt is paid, his guilt will have been absolved to some extent. It can never be entirely resolved in this manner, of course, since the basis for the guilt is unconscious, but punishments for specific delinquent acts can relieve his sense of guilt momentarily by creating a situation of punishment and forgiveness.

The crystallized delinquent will not be inclined to commit the usual kind of impulsive delinquencies, i.e., theft, vandalism, or illicit sexual relations. Instead, since his difficulties stem largely from interpersonal conflicts, he will tend to focus upon offenses that in one way or another portray the "moral superiority" of the offender and the "moral degradation" of the antagonist. His delinquencies, therefore, will tend to approximate religious crusades against heretical, immoral foes.

Clearly, then, since delinquency serves as a convenient way to reduce unconscious guilt, to express conscious irritations toward enemies, and to proclaim forthrightly a disenchantment with legitimate society, it knits together many emotions and sentiments that would otherwise mean this delinquent's banishment from all social intercourse and his personal disorganization. Delinquency, then, offers such an individual an identity that confirms his conscious needs and gives them direction. In E. H. Erikson's terms, it provides a negative identity.[39]

Symptomatic Delinquency

The third general class of delinquents, the symptomatic delinquent, utilizes delinquent behavior in a manner that is essentially different from either the impulsive delinquent or the neurotic delinquent. Whereas the neurotic delinquent uses it to relieve guilt feelings and to express vengeful attitudes, the symptomatic delinquent uses delinquency primarily as a means of expressing unconscious sexual and aggressive needs in highly symbolic ways. He does not ordinarily express these unconscious needs directly in activities that are obviously sexual or aggressive; rather, he expresses them metaphorically in activities that are only distantly related to the actual nature of his unconscious needs.

Although the unconscious appreciates the significance of his activities, the conventional person who witnesses his behavior and even the delinquent himself may not consciously understand its true significance. The symptomatic delinquent, therefore, does not act out anti-social motives in the same sense that the impulsive delinquent does, since the unconscious impulses at the root of his delinquent behavior are not directly expressed in action—they must be disguised before they can be expressed consciously. Neither, however, does he use delinquency in a desperate effort to rid himself of noxious emotions as the inadequate delinquent does. Most generally, he accidentally stumbles upon an activity that happens to be significant to his unconscious needs; and because it provides an uncanny satisfaction, he is unable to resist returning to the activity again and again.

Aside from his unquenchable need to perform the symptomatic act over and over, this kind of delinquent presents a distinctly ordinary and even banal picture. He is capable of warm, positive relationships with others; he does have inhibitions of a conventional sort; and he does feel ashamed and remorseful for his actions.

The Cleptomaniac

The cleptomaniac, for example, is typically a young woman for whom stealing has come unconsciously to symbolize the recovery of a prized possession that was unjustly taken from her.[40] The origin of this feeling can in individual cases be found at any of several points in the person's development, but in many cases the lost object is a missing penis, and stealing represents the desire to compensate for an unconscious sense of injustice and loss. Stealing is a particularly appropriate reaction for such individuals because it represents symbolically both retribution for the previous injury and a recovery of the lost object. Since it is expressive of unconscious needs on two counts, it is a simple matter for the ego to persuade itself momentarily at least that the theft is morally justified. But once the deed has been completed, the individual's conventional inhibitions usually revive, and he experiences considerable anxiety and guilt.

The Pyromaniac

A second type of symptomatic delinquency that is equally well known is pyromania. The pyromaniac is driven to set fires because conflagrations and their consequences express something in the unconscious that cannot be discharged adequately in any other way. According to Ernst Simmel, the pyromaniac is typically a young man who suffers from massive inhibitions regarding genital sexuality but who at the same time is able to derive considerable sexual satisfaction from urethral activities, i.e., urination and retention of the urine.[41] The inability to express his sexual needs genitally means that this young man's urges will eventually become rather strong, and his ability to derive pleasure from urethral activities means that flowing liquids will assume a peculiar significance to his unconscious. Fire, of course, does have a fluid quality about it; but even more important, the effort to extinguish fires usually involves great streams of water. Thus, according to Simmel, the pyromaniac sets fires compulsively because the efforts of firemen to put them out provide him with an immensely exciting spectacle that is directly analogous to his own preferred mode of sexual gratification. Although he may sincerely desire to resist the temptation, he is powerless before the press of his unconscious to recapture the sensations that are associated with the fires.

The Sexual Delinquent

A third type of symptomatic delinquent, whom we shall label the sexual delinquent, is distinguished by the fact that the unconscious needs at the root of his delinquency center in an intense dread of being castrated. This fear can be consciously expressed in many ways, but in general there are three major patterns—fetishism, exhibitionism, and voyeurism. The first of these patterns, fetishism, is usually found in males and represents an attempt to gain reassurance that the paternal threat of castration need not be taken seriously.[42] One way of removing castration as a realistic threat is to establish that there are very few who have ever suffered it. The delinquent who indulges in fetishism, therefore, does so to prove to himself that women do, indeed, possess a penis and that the threat of castration is in general an empty one. To the delinquent, the stolen article symbolizes the feminine penis and confirms that many women do possess a male organ. The unconscious, of course, forms associations between the penis and all kinds of objects, and the nature of these associations is usually idiosyncratic to the person, depending upon his peculiar experience. For example, one individual might unconsciously associate a shoe with the penis, whereas another might relate it to a hat or a handkerchief. The specific article that is repeatedly stolen will depend largely on the individual's unique experience, but whatever the specific nature of the fetish, its function is to relieve the delinquent's castration fears by reaffirming to the unconscious that women do possess a penis.

The same kind of unconscious tension seems also to be at the root of exhibitionism and voyeurism.[43] The male exhibitionist typically startles females by revealing himself so that through their fear or disgust the potency of his genitals is reaffirmed. The voyeur, on the other hand, attempts to witness scenes similar to those that gave rise to his unconscious anxieties so that he will eventually be able to master the emotions they induced. But because the basis of these feelings is unconscious, there is very little hope that the voyeur will in the end be able to control his anxieties in this way.

As viewed by Fenichel, fetishism, exhibitionism, and voyeurism are aberrations that can be traced back to childish fears of castration. It would appear, therefore, that a given individual might well express his unconscious desires in any of these three delinquent patterns and that circumstances dictate which pattern will be selected at a given time. Although legal statutes may require a distinction between these three patterns, to psychoanalytic theory they are all variations of the same basic type.

Conclusion

With this discussion of the symptomatic delinquent we have completed our consideration of the psychological typology of delinquency. We have attempted to discover the psychological basis of delinquency, and in the course of this analysis we have uncovered three distinct psychological processes. Although conceptually these processes are mutually exclusive, empirically some of them can occur together. The inadequate delinquent, for example, presents a syndrome of difficulties that might very well be experienced by other types as they become more deeply embroiled with the police, the courts, and the training schools. The symptomatic delinquent in particular should be vulnerable to the anxieties of the inadequate delinquent.

The impulsive delinquent, however, could never exhibit the same characteristics as the symptomatic delinquent, since to be one necessarily precludes being the other. The symptomatic delinquent is compelled by unconscious motives to behave in a delinquent way, but the existence of unconscious motives implies also the existence of a vigilant superego, which, in turn, implies that the direct acting-out of primitive motives is highly unlikely. Hence, symptomatic delinquency and impulsive delinquency are not likely to appear in the same adolescent.

It is probably true, moreover, that crystallized delinquency, when it does appear, represents a rather advanced stage in the career of most delinquents. The adolescent must have been exposed to persistent condemnation, and he must also have come to appreciate the psychic advantages of a delinquent career. It takes a specific kind of experience to become a crystallized delinquent, and this experience in itself implies a fairly lengthy career as a delinquent. It is conceivable, then, that certain types of impulsive delinquents—those types whose character structure is relatively intact—could advance into this stage as their guilt became more profound.

There are, then, several ways in which these processes can blend together in specific individuals to shape their behavior. It should be clear, nevertheless, that these types are analytically distinct, since they are all based on distinctive constellations of psychological forces.

In addition to being analytically distinct, it also appears that these three classes exhaust the range of possibilities contained within psychoanalytic theory. In general, there are three functions that must be considered in describing the individual's personality: the intensity and orientation of his libidinal energy, the strength of his ego, and the nature of his superego. When the superego is rudimentary or primitive, libidinal energy need not be radically transformed as it is translated into behavior; and for this reason, a primitive or immature superego often means a primitive motive structure as well. Our first class, the impulsive delinquent, corresponds to this combination. Furthermore, it is possible to combine repressed libidinal needs that form the basis for unconventional, if not anti-social, behavior with an ego and superego that have developed in relatively normal ways, and the result in this case is our symptomatic delinquent.

And, finally, when the ego is threatened by alien and noxious emotions, it may turn to delinquent action in an irrational and uncontrolled attempt to purge itself, or it may utilize delinquency as a way of repressing and relieving these disruptive emotions.

Thus, the ego may be forced into delinquent behavior by neurotic adjustments in the adolescent's personality. Thus, we have considered every function of the personality, and we have identified a general class of delinquents that arises when one or more of these functions is pathological. There are, then, just three psychological classes of delinquents, and these three classes embrace the full range of classes that are possible in psychoanalytic theory.

This is not to suggest that every type of delinquency that can exist within this framework has been isolated. These three classes must themselves be further refined and clarified before we have completed our assignment, but it is clear that the broad outlines of a psychological typology are now in sight. In terms of the criteria laid down in Chapter Three regarding ideal typologies, therefore, this typology measures up reasonably well.

We might also evaluate it by comparing it with several well known typologies that were not considered in its original formulation. Certainly, one of the most widely discussed typologies to appear in recent years is that developed by the Gluecks describing three somatotypes. Their endomorphic delinquent seems to correspond quite closely to the self-centered indulged type, while the ectomorphic delinquent bears some resemblance to the crystallized delinquent. The mesomorphic delinquent also is similar in certain respects to the unsocialized aggressive child, although he does not appear to be so violent or vicious. Hewitt and Jenkins also describe two types that can be located in the above typology. Their unsocialized aggressive child, of course, corresponds to the type with the same name, and the overinhibited child may represent the inadequate delinquent at an early, nondelinquent stage in his development. Their socialized delinquent, however, corresponds to the cultural delinquent described by other theorists and does not belong to this typology.

Reiss has also proposed a typology of delinquency based upon Freudian theory, *viz.,* the delinquent with markedly weak ego controls, the delinquent with relatively defective superego controls, and the relatively integrated delinquent.[44] The first type probably describes our inadequate delinquent, and the second probably corresponds to the entire impulsive class. The third type is the familiar cultural delinquent.

In conclusion, then, it would appear that the typology offered in this chapter does anticipate the types mentioned by the most prominent researchers who have recently given some attention to this general problem. It does appear, therefore, to be comprehensive as I have already suggested. Moreover, it attempts to classify the types genotypically in terms of their psychodynamic processes, and it seeks to refine the types within the three general classes to the point where they can be accurately applied to individuals. All in all, then, this typology is comprehensive; it attempts to bring the descriptions of the types to a fairly high resolve; and it attempts to group those types together that are genotypically similar.

NOTES

[1] Sigmund Freud, "Some Character-Types Met with in Psycho-analytic Work," *Collected Papers,* Vol. IV, 1925, pp. 324–44.

[2] Freud, "Libidinal Types," *ibid.,* Vol. V, 1950, pp. 247–50.

[3] Franz Alexander and Hugo Staub, *The Criminal, the Judge, and the Public* (New York: Free Press, 1956), pp. 83–124.

[4] *Ibid.*, pp. 119–20.

[5] *Ibid.*, pp. 120–21.

[6] *Ibid.*, p. 121.

[7] *Ibid.*, pp. 121–23.

[8] *Ibid.*, p. 123.

[9] This type seems to resemble Glover's functional delinquent. See Edward Glover, "On the Desirability of Isolating a 'Functional' Group of Delinquent Disorders," *British Journal of Delinquency*, Vol. 1, No. 1 (1950), pp. 104–12.

[10] See either of the following works by David Abrahamsen, *Crime and the Human Mind* (New York: Columbia University Press, 1944), pp. 94–96; or *Psychology of Crime* (New York: Columbia University Press, 1960), pp. 123–27.

[11] See either of the following: Abrahamsen, *Psychology of Crime*, pp. 127–34; or *Who Are the Guilty?* (New York: Grove Press, 1952), pp. 149–54.

[12] Abrahamsen, *Psychology of Crime*, pp. 134–44.

[13] *Ibid.*, pp. 144–50.

[14] Abrahamsen, *Crime and the Human Mind*, pp. 125–26.

[15] Kate Friedlander, *The Psychoanalytic Approach to Juvenile Delinquency* (New York: International Universities Press, 1947), pp. 78–94.

[16] *Ibid.*, pp. 84–89.

[17] *Ibid.*, pp. 116–17.

[18] *Ibid.*, pp. 123–48.

[19] *Ibid.*, pp. 178–82.

[20] *Ibid.*, pp. 186–87.

[21] *Ibid.*, pp. 143–48.

[22] *Ibid.*, p. 187.

[23] R. Nevitt Sanford, "A Psychoanalytic Study of Three Criminal Types," *Journal of Criminal Psychopathology*, Vol. 5, No. 1 (July, 1943), pp. 57–68.

24 S. Kirson Weinberg, *Society and Personality Disorders* (Englewood Cliffs: Prentice-Hall, 1952), pp. 264–69.

25 *Ibid.,* pp. 270–79.

26 *Ibid.,* pp. 281–85.

27 *Ibid.,* pp. 285–86.

28 *Ibid.,* p. 288.

29 Lester E. Hewitt and Richard L. Jenkins, *Fundamental Patterns of Maladjustment* (Springfield, Illinois: State Printer, 1947), pp. 34–42.

30 See Margaret S. Mahler, "Les 'Enfants Terribles'," in K. R. Eissler, ed., *Searchlights on Delinquency* (New York: International Universities Press, 1949), pp. 77–89; David Levy, *Maternal Overprotection* (New York: Columbia University Press, 1948), pp. 159–99; and Sheldon and Eleanor Glueck, *Physique and Delinquency* (New York: Harper & Row, 1956), pp. 228–34.

31 It is likely that Lee Harvey Oswald would fit within this category.

32 Mahler, " 'Les Enfants Terribles'," pp. 83–88. See also Wilhelm Reich, *Character Analysis,* 3d ed. (New York: Orgone Institute Press, 1949), pp. 200–7.

33 Otto Fenichel, *The Psychoanalytic Theory of Neurosis* (New York: Norton, 1945), pp. 374–75; and Weinberg, *Society,* pp. 274–75.

34 Fenichel, *Psychoanalytic Theory,* pp. 331–32.

35 For three valuable descriptions of the nature of ego-diffusion see Erik Erikson's, "The Problem of Ego Identity," *Journal of American Psychoanalytic Association,* Vol. 4, No. 1 (1956), pp. 51–121; Fritz Redl and David Wineman, *Children Who Hate* (Glencoe: Free Press, 1951), Chapters II, III, IV, and V; and Hyman Grossbard, "Ego-deficiency in Delinquents," *Social Casework,* Vol. XLIII, No. 4 (1962), pp. 171–78.

36 See pp. 155, 161, 171, 175, for a discussion of these analyses.

37 The only mention of this type in the typologies discussed earlier is Sanford's discussion of the anti-social criminal. See pp. 171–72.

38 Erik Erikson, "Identity and the Life Cycle," *Psychological Issues,* Monograph 1, Vol. 1, No. 1 (1959), pp. 129–32.

39 *Ibid.,* pp. 122–29.

40 Fenichel, *Psychoanalytic Theory,* pp. 370–71.

41 Ernst Simmel, "Incendiarism," in K. R. Eissler, ed., *Searchlights on Delinquency,* pp. 90–101.

42 Fenichel, *Psychoanalytic Theory,* pp. 370–71.

43 *Ibid.,* p. 105.

44 Albert J. Reiss, "Social Correlates of Psychological Types of Delinquency," *American Sociological Review,* Vol. 17, No. 6 (December, 1952), pp. 710–18; and his "Delinquency as the Failure of Personal and Social Controls," *American Sociological Review,* Vol. 16, No. 2 (April, 1951), pp. 196–207.

CHAPTER 6

Toward a Synthetic Typology of Delinquency

In Chapter Three we saw that it is necessary if we are to formulate a definitive explanation of delinquent behavior to cast our arguments in the form of ideal typologies and to articulate these typologies by means of Lewinian field theory into a comprehensive, synthetic typology of delinquency. As it was originally developed, Lewinian field theory primarily focused upon the explanation of individual action in terms of psychological forces, but in this discussion I have sought to extend field theory by introducing social forces as causal factors and by focusing upon the social action of groups as well as individuals.

Clearly, the action of individuals and the action of groups are intimately interrclated, and to understand one it is in general necessary to take into account the other. Moreover, since both are aspects of action, the same logical framework, i.e., field theory, is applicable to each. Just as it is possible to develop explanations of individual action by considering the life-space as the arena wherein psychological forces mold and manipulate socially based perceptions; so, too, it is possible to explain the action of a group by considering the situation as the site wherein the group's structure adjusts to the exigencies of the immediate environment. The concepts of the life-space and the situation, therefore, are similar in that they both represent a stage upon which dynamic, social psychological dramas are enacted. It is easy to overlook the continuous adjustment of groups to their situations by limiting one's attention myopically to the individual, but it is probably true that little significant change is ever achieved except by the adjustment of groups to their situations. The action of groups, therefore, is directly analogous to that of individuals and requires for its analysis a field theoretical framework.

Indeed, it is possible using the same ideal typologies to construct a synthetic typology of group action as well as one of individual action. Thus, when the forces described by social and psychological typologies converge in the context of an individual's life-space, the result is a typology of individual action; but when these same forces come together in a situation, a typology of group action is the result. We are obliged, therefore, to develop in this chapter two typologies of delinquent action: one in which the individual's action is described from the standpoint of his life-space; and the other in which the group's reaction to its situation is charted with special attention to the types of individuals that are likely to compose the group. Let us proceed by considering first the synthetic typology of individual delinquent action.

A Synthetic Typology of Delinquent Individuals

In developing a synthetic typology of individual delinquency, it is necessary to indicate how the forces in the individual's psychological field interact with his perceptions of the immediate social situation. It must be remembered, however, that these factors do not combine in an arbitrary or mechanical fashion to shape the individual's life-space. Rather, those aspects of the situation that are meaningful to his psychological field are singled out in the life-space for special elaboration, whereas those that are not are largely ignored. Moreover, the mere fact of being accepted—or rejected—in a situation often has a profound effect upon the individual's personality, focusing and sharpening his predispositions—or, alternatively, confounding and diffusing them. Thus, in formulating our descriptions of the typical life-space underlying a delinquent action, we must be especially alert to homologies that exist between the psychological fields of typical delinquents and the typical situations they confront.[1]

Beginning with the unsocialized aggressive child, it would seem that his ungoverned, anti-social personality would forbid a smooth adjustment to any type of structured situation. Thus, the mild demands that the mischievous-indulgent pattern in the upper upper-class makes of its members are sufficient to eliminate all possibility of his adapting to the pattern. He could not restrain himself for the sake of good form, and even if he could, he would have little capacity for sensing what is stylistic and what is not. The primitive, infantile character of his personality, therefore, provides little basis for his conforming even minimally to the delinquent pattern of the upper upper-class. Thus, in the upper upper-class he would be recognized quite early even by his peers as seriously anti-social; and until he were institutionalized by his parents or other responsible adults, his life would be a lonely, isolated one.

Superficially, at least, it might seem that the impulsive quality of his behavior would fit more consistently with the aggressive-exploitative delinquent pattern of the lower upper- and upper middle-classes. Here, the unsocialized aggressive child is presented with a set of values that corresponds to some extent with his own peculiar inclination to violent, egocentric behavior. But just as the members of these cliques are expected to go all out in the pursuit of individualistic goals, they are also expected to accept the authority of the clique, something the unsocialized aggressive child could never do consistently. Thus, even if his behavior were acceptable for a time among the delinquents of these classes, his consistently vicious, egocentric orientation would offend even their sensibilities and ultimately lead to his expulsion from their cliques. As in the upper upper-class he is likely to be seen as deeply pathological by his peers in this class and to steer a lonely, delinquent course until responsible adults finally see to his institutionalization.

The upper lower-class, however, is likely to be somewhat more hospitable to the unsocialized aggressive child. There is a good chance, for example, that the conflict pattern occasionally found in this class would be compatible with his peculiar style. Although he would experience considerable difficulty in submitting to the discipline and highly authoritarian structure of the fighting gang, his reputation for fearlessness might well compensate for his other deficiencies; and in really vicious gangs, it could even carry him to a position of leadership. Most often, however, his irrational, explosive disposition would relegate him to an anomalous position in these gangs. The members of the gang would respect him for his "heart," but at the same time they would sense the depth of his pathology and avoid intimate association with him.[2]

Similarly, his reception by the theft gang in this class would be reasonably cordial. Its casual structure would place few restrictions on his behavior, and while he would have little direct interest in many of the gang's more juvenile activities—theft, gambling, and drinking as forms of excitement—his violently explosive manner would command a certain respect among the members of the gang. He probably would not form many close friends within the gang, but his fighting ability would earn him the right to associate loosely with the gang as long as it suited his purposes.

There is, however, little chance that he would be accepted into the criminal pattern as it ordinarily develops in upper lower-class neighborhoods. It demands a selfless dedication to criminal values and a technical finesse that are simply beyond the capacities of the unsocialized aggressive child. He could never exercise the control over himself that the criminal pattern requires, nor could he interest himself in the necessary but routine techniques of criminal behavior. Hence, his irresponsibility and clumsiness would quickly mark him as unacceptable to the members of this pattern and, in the absence of other types of delinquent gangs, force him into isolation.

Due to the nature of the disorganized acting-out pattern in the lower lower-class, he would not encounter significant pressure to conform to any particular normative structure; and for this reason, his acting-out tendencies would not be regarded as especially noteworthy or unusual. His violent personality, however, would still constitute a menace to those around him; and on this account, the members of this class would give him a wide berth. In the lower lower-class, then, he would find an opportunity to behave pretty much as he desires, although here as in the other classes he would neither seek nor find acceptance and companionship.

It is clear that the native inclinations of the unsocialized aggressive child are generally in opposition to the values and norms of most of the delinquent patterns that he is likely to encounter. With the possible exception of the conflict pattern, he experiences at least avoidance and occasionally suppression at the hands of his fellow delinquents. He is most at home in the upper lower-class conflict pattern, but even here his integration with the gang is on a formal rather than a personal basis. Thus, the unsocialized aggressive child can follow one of two paths, depending upon the nature of the situation within which he finds himself. If he happens to live in an upper lower-class neighborhood that supports a conflict pattern of delinquency, he is likely to become an active participant in its violence against other groups and to adjust in a reforming fashion to the situation. He will, in this case, approximate Yablonsky's description of the core members of fighting gangs in Manhattan.[3] In any other neighborhood, his delinquent activities will be carried on largely alone or in the company of casual acquaintances, and his adjustment would conform to the withdrawn mode.

The self-centered indulged delinquent should adapt somewhat more flexibly to the situations he confronts. His greater warmth and charm mean that he will form friendships somewhat more easily, and his resourcefulness and self-confidence mean that he will often move to a leadership position in the groups to which he belongs. Thus, we can expect that this lad will be welcomed considerably more readily into teenage delinquent groups than the unsocialized aggressive child.

The delinquent pattern that is most congruent with his own peculiar inclinations is unquestionably the aggressive-exploitative pattern of the lower upper- and upper middle-classes. Here, there is ample latitude for him to express his combative urges against rival cliques and individuals; and at the same time, he is encouraged to strive for and win the favors of his feminine classmates, two activities that are quite meaningful to the self-centered indulged delinquent. Moreover, since the Dionysian ethos of these cliques fits so well with his own personality style, we might expect that he would frequently play an important role in formulating the values of aggressive-exploitative cliques in those communities where they have not yet emerged in clear form.

His own sexual successes, for example, might inspire other members to engage in similar pursuits, while his personal differences with other teenagers might form the basis for systematic rivalries among several neighboring cliques. Thus, the aggressive-exploitative pattern, which is itself a product of broad social forces, happens to invite and endorse just those activities that the self-centered indulged delinquent finds most gratifying. If this pattern is already well established in the community structure, it will merely provide the framework within which this boy can achieve a meaningful and fulfilling career as an adolescent. If it is present only in latent form, this youngster will play a major role in fostering its emergence in the community.

This same boy can also be expected to adapt reasonably well to the upper lower-class conflict pattern.

His resourcefulness would provide a versatility that is often missing in fighting gangs, and his volatile, assertive manner would be sufficient to establish and maintain his authority over all but the most unsocialized of his peers.[5] Nevertheless, since violence is not the only or even the principal focus of his personality, we might anticipate that, if conditions permitted, he would seek to broaden the gang's repertoire to include other kinds of activities in addition to those it usually pursues. We might expect the gang to pay greater heed to the opposite sex under his leadership. And to enliven the repetitive routine that characterizes the activities of such gangs, he could be expected to initiate certain exotic forms of vandalism and theft. Under his tutelage, then, the fighting gang might well be slowly transformed into the more common upper lower-class theft pattern. No such metamorphosis could occur, of course, if a lessening of intergroup tension in the neighborhood did not invite it; but if conditions were ripe for such a change, the thirst for variety and the imagination of the self-centered indulged child would hasten and facilitate it.

It is apparent that the lower upper-class theft pattern offers the self-centered indulged delinquent considerable scope for developing the full range of his interests and emotions. Its cliques and gangs are less authoritarian and focused than those in the conflict pattern; hence, he will be much freer to pursue whatever strikes his fancy. Although he is not a coward, he does not thrive on violence as some other types do; and when confronted with continual threat and aggression, he tends to become bored and sour. The variety and the relatively amorphous character of the theft pattern suit his particular needs quite well, and he can be expected to fit smoothly into this pattern.[6]

His adjustment to the criminal pattern, however, is not likely to prove so simple. To be sure, his charm, resourcefulness, and ascendency make him an attractive candidate for any group; but once in the criminal gang, there is reason to expect that he would not feel perfectly comfortable. The rigid self-discipline that is expected of criminally oriented delinquents would cramp his natural volatility, and the complex organization of mature criminal gangs would tend to conflict with his desires for immediate gratification. But perhaps the greatest obstacle to his full participation in the criminal gang is his inability to accept, or even adjust, to the authority of older, overbearing males. Since many professional criminals enjoy ostentatious displays of wealth and power, the self-centered indulged delinquent can be depended upon to reject them as individuals and to repudiate them as leaders. All in all, then, he is likely to regard the structure of the criminal pattern as too restricting and its apprenticeship status vis-à-vis adult criminals too humiliating for his own tastes.

His adjustment within the lower lower-class delinquent pattern, however, would be simple enough. His exploitativeness and his impatience with delay would not be regarded as especially unusual, and since his viciousness emerges only when confronted with restricting persons or circumstances, it would often appear justified to the members of this class. There is, moreover, little to excite his personal displeasure in this class. His combativeness and fertile imagination would be regarded as strengths by his peers, and in the absence of pressure to curb his more exploitative appetites, he would in general react positively to the rather unstructured situation within which he found himself. The self-centered indulged delinquent, then, would feel quite comfortable in the disorganized act-ing-out pattern of the lower lower-class.

The delinquent pattern that would present the greatest difficulty to this type of boy is the mischievous-indulgent pattern of the upper upper-class. Although he would be recognized as a boy with considerable style, his exploitativeness and violent temper would brand him as basically anti-social and, therefore, unfit for the company of his more normal peers. Hence, in the upper upper-class his repeated violations of the rights and sensibilities of others would lead eventually to his isolation and categorization as a neurotic or delinquent.

All in all, then, the self-centered indulged delin-quent is likely to adapt fairly well to four of the six delinquent patterns as we described them in Chapter Four. He combines in his personality a charm and resourcefulness that are fundamental to good surface relations with others and a capacity for violence and callous exploitation that is essential for a convincing performance of delinquency roles. Thus, he is admir-ably suited for a reforming role in most delinquent patterns that are relatively unstructured.

Moving on to the psychopathic delinquent, it would seem that in contrast to the self-centered indulged child, he would adjust to the delinquent patterns of the several classes with considerable difficulty. His irresponsibility would throw him into repeated con-flict wtih his peers, and his shallow, opportunistic orientation would render the companionship of the gang meaningless as far as he was concerned. There is good reason, therefore, to anticipate that this boy could not associate for any length of time with the more highly structured delinquent patterns where each member's obligations to his peers are well understood. He might, through force of circumstances, submit to the discipline of one of these gangs for a time, but it would have little meaning for him; and when the crisis had passed, he would move out on his own again.

The upper upper-class emphasis upon style and good form, for example, would appear to the psychopathic delinquent as artificial and unimportant. Accordingly, he would attach little significance to membership in cliques pursuing a mischievous-indulgent pattern. Similarly, he would not appreciate the importance of demonstrating one's ability through competition, since for him nothing is worth such strenuous effort. Consequently, the aggressive-exploitative delinquent pattern of the lower upper- and upper middle-classes would hold little attraction.

His inability to honor socially imposed obligations would also prevent his adapting successfully to the criminal and conflict patterns of the upper lower-class. The satisfaction that comes with perfecting one's skill —even if it involves criminal techniques—is lost on this young man; and although he can be extremely cruel to others, violence is not a value worthy of continuous elaboration. Thus, he would regard the criminal and conflict patterns with utter indifference. He might find the theft pattern of the upper lower-class more relevant to his own needs, since it makes few demands upon its members. But even here his indifference toward the feelings and opinions of others would lead to strained relations with his fellow delinquents and to his ultimate exclusion from the group.

The only pattern that might prove compatible with his irresponsible orientation is the disorganized acting-out pattern of the lower lower-class. Here he would confront a minimum of restraint and coercion, leaving him free to behave much as he desires. He would not form any close friendships among his peers in this pattern, but neither would he be systematically denounced and condemned in the manner that is his lot in the cliques of the higher classes. Thus, it would seem that the psychopathic delinquent is likely to shun most structured patterns of delinquency and to pursue his egocentric needs largely in social isolation. But since withdrawal is quite consistent with his own preferences, he would generally feel little distress in his solitude.

The sexual pervert presents a special problem. Since his type of anti-social behavior is as unacceptable to his delinquent peers as it is to society, he will generally find it necessary to conceal his perversion from other delinquents. But insofar as he is successful in this regard, his anti-social behavior, i.e., homosexuality, becomes irrelevant to his adjustment to a delinquent pattern. His adjustment to a delinquent situation, therefore, must be assessed as if his own particular needs and inhibitions were largely irrelevant to the requirements of the pattern in question. Thus, if he can conceal his abnormality, he will conform to the six delinquent patterns described in Chapter Four much as the normal adolescent does, i.e., without distinction.

His chances of concealing his perversion, however, are not good. Four of the six social patterns of delinquency, i.e., the aggressive-exploitative pattern and the criminal, fighting, and theft patterns of the upper lower-class, place a heavy emphasis upon masculinity and success with the opposite sex. The homosexual, of course, would find it difficult to fulfill these requirements; and even if there were no overt evidence of his perversion, overtones would probably creep into his relations with his peers that in the end would repel them. Hence, it is not likely that a homosexual adolescent would gain admission to these four delinquent patterns with any significant frequency.

In the mischievous-indulgent pattern he would not encounter the same difficulties, since the emphasis upon masculinity is much less vigorous there. If he did not express his perversion overtly, he would probably not encounter much difficulty in adapting adequately to the delinquent patterns of this class. The upper upper-class, however, is no more tolerant of sexual perversion than the other classes; and if he were to take advantage of his acceptance in the cliques of this class to indulge his perversion, he would be rejected by his peers and expelled from their groups.

In the lower lower-class, however, he might find a certain tolerance for his abnormality and an opportunity to practice it openly. The typical lower lower-class person is rarely surprised at the deviant eccentricities of his associates; and, consequently, the sexual pervert could find a degree of acceptance and even companionship in this class.[7]

The inadequate delinquent would also encounter difficulty in adapting to the social patterns of delinquency. His disorganized, diffuse manner is incompatible with any normative pattern that requires even a modest degree of self-control and assertiveness. As a delinquent, therefore, he has little to look forward to save rejection and ridicule. In the upper upper-class, for example, his lack of self-esteem and his inability to focus his behavior would afford little basis for winning the respect of adolescents in the mischievous-indulgent pattern. Hence, in this class he would be forced to carry out his delinquent activities largely alone. In the lower upper- and upper middle-classes, he would be ignored as awkward and incompetent—as incapable of participating in the exploitative-aggressive delinquent pattern—and in the upper lower-class his timidity and fearfulness would only attract a merciless scapegoating.[8]

Only in the lower lower-class would he find a surcease from torment and rejection. Since a considerable portion of his peers would also exhibit symptoms of inadequacy, he would probably find a sympathy or at least a tolerance here that was not exhibited in the higher classes. Thus, the absence of oppressive demands, together with the understanding that he finds in this class, will render his conforming to the disorganized acting-out pattern relatively easy.

The symptomatic delinquent would also experience a varying success in adapting to the delinquent patterns of the various classes. The cleptomaniac, for example, might well find a certain audience among his peers in the upper upper-class. Since there is in this class a casual disregard for property, to his peers his compulsive stealing would seem quaint—especially if he accomplished it with a degree of finesse. Thus, a mild cleptomaniac might find acceptance and approval in a mischievous-indulgent clique. Chronic, uncontrolled stealing, however, would be seen by his companions as pathological, and the cleptomaniac with an overwhelming desire to steal would probably not find a place in the adolescent cliques of this class.

The chronic cleptomaniac would encounter much the same fate in several of the other classes as well. His peers in the lower upper- and upper middle-classes would assess his compulsion accurately, and if he were not otherwise distinctive or outstanding, they would have very little to do with him. In the conflict and criminal patterns of the upper lower-class, his stealing would appear at best bizarre and at worst embarrassing to the interests of the gang. Hence, even if he were accepted within these gangs, he would probably be ridiculed for his compulsion.

In the theft pattern, however, he might be tolerated. His concentration upon theft at the expense of other delinquent activities endorsed by the gang would stigmatize him to some extent in the eyes of his fellows, but the casual structure of these cliques allows a greater tolerance of eccentric individuals, and his repetitive stealing would at least qualify him for membership. In the lower lower-class, his compulsion to steal would not be regarded as seriously abnormal; and, accordingly, he would find many companions who gave little attention to this quirk in his personality.

The pyromaniac, however, would not find much tolerance among his fellow adolescents. Setting disastrous fires would be too obviously anti-social to win the approval of his upper upper-class peers, including those committed to the mischievous-indulgent pattern of delinquency. Mild forms of theft and vandalism are one thing, but setting fires in which people die and great property damage results is quite another. Insofar as he were known, the pyromaniac would be regarded by the youngsters as a definite menace, and few would have anything to do with him. He would also be viewed in much the same way in the lower upper- and upper middle-classes. Arson does not qualify as an adolescent prank among the members of the aggressive-exploitative delinquent pattern, and, accordingly, the pyromaniac would be avoided by the members of these cliques.

In the upper lower-class he would get a mixed reception. In the criminal and theft patterns, his behavior would appear pointless; but in the conflict pattern, his eccentricity might be integrated into the group's structure as another weapon in the gang's armamentarium. Thus, the pyromaniac might be held in reserve as a "secret weapon" and used by a fighting gang to destroy the meeting places of its rivals. In any case, the seriousness of his delinquency would not act as an obstacle to his participation in the conflict pattern; and, depending upon the degree to which he were able to refine and focus his pyromania, he might be utilized by the gang for its own ends.

In the lower lower-class, fire is always a serious threat; and if his pyromania were known, he would certainly be regarded by his peers as a serious problem. Other delinquents, to be sure, would not take vigorous exception to his behavior, but neither would they be inclined to join or support him in it. Thus, in the lower lower-class he would be shunned and perhaps even expelled from adolescent cliques if his behavior became too dangerous. The pyromaniac, then, would be an isolate in every class with the possible exception of the upper lower-class, where he might be admitted to the conflict pattern, if he could find ways of bringing his compulsion under the discipline of the gang.

The sexual delinquents—those delinquents who are obsessed with fetishism, exhibitionism, or voyeurism—will also fare differently in the several classes. There is a certain amount of this kind of behavior among adolescents at all levels, and, as a result, this type of delinquent, particularly if his compulsion is mild, would not seem too unusual to his fellows. If his behavior were obviously compulsive, however, the whole picture would change considerably.

In the upper classes, for example, a pattern of uncontrolled sexual aberration would be recognized for what it is, mental pathology, and its author would not be highly regarded by his peers. In the lower classes, he would be viewed as eccentric but not necessarily as abnormal or mentally deranged. If he became especially skilled, at voyeurism, for example, he might serve as a diversion for his compatriots in the upper lower-class theft pattern and in the lower lower-class disorganized acting-out pattern. Delinquents in the other patterns, including those in the upper-classes, would regard his actions as too bizarre to merit serious attention.

In sum, then, the symptomatic delinquent can adjust to a delinquent pattern in one of two ways. If his compulsion is outrageous to the members of a particular pattern, he has no choice but to pursue his unusual desires in isolation. If his compulsion is consistent with the values and/or objectives of the pattern, he will be accepted into the cliques of that pattern. But since his compulsion is inflexible and insensitive to the exigencies of the situation, his role in the clique will at best be only marginal. Thus, even though he may become a member of a delinquent clique, his influence upon its structure will still be minimal.

Since the crystallized delinquent exhibits an unusually strong commitment to delinquent behavior, unlike many other delinquent types, his ability to accept the restrictions of a delinquent social pattern is considerable. For him, the kind of delinquency is not important as long as it is defiantly delinquent. Because it is important that his protest be recognized as such by the community, he would disdain those patterns that are not defiantly anti-social—the mischievous-indulgent pattern and the exploitative-aggressive patterns—as childish and not worthy of his attention. He would, on the other hand, appreciate the criminal and conflict patterns of the upper lower-class as systematically and genuinely delinquent.

His planning and organizing ability, his rigid self-control, and his sensitive appreciation of his fellow delinquents fit him quite well for a career in organized crime. Indeed, when he appears in neighborhoods where the criminal pattern exists, he will soon find his way into these gangs and eventually into a leadership position.[9] He lacks the imagination and resourcefulness of the self-centered indulged delinquent, but he possesses an uncommon self-discipline and a dedication to criminal values that more than compensates for these deficiencies. Thus, whereas his leadership would not be brilliant, it would be steady and dependable, and his seemingly mature manner would inspire respect among his fellow delinquents. He would bring to the criminal gang the discipline and purposefulness it needs to advance quickly into organized crime, while organized crime for its part would provide him with a convenient means for displaying his defiance of society and his repudiation of its values. His presence, therefore, would have a reforming effect upon the gang and its structure.

Much the same compatibility would also be observed between the crystallized delinquent and the upper lower-class conflict pattern. Here, too, the opportunity to express his deep hatred toward conventional groups and institutions could not be ignored;

and as a result, if this pattern existed in his neighborhood, he would be drawn into its structure and feel quite comfortable there. He might be repelled by the wanton, uncontrolled activities of some extremely vicious gangs, but he would delight in the opportunity to demonstrate his own lack of respect for conventional groups. Thus, he would encourage the gang to pursue a defiantly anti-social pattern directed against, perhaps, the police and other representatives of the dominant power groups in the neighborhood rather than a randomly vicious pattern against other adolescent gangs and innocent bystanders.[10] All in all, then, his membership in the gang would mean that it would become relatively focused and that it would move inexorably toward serious criminal involvement with the police, courts, and correctional institutions of the community.

The absence of a deep anti-social commitment in the theft pattern of the upper lower-class would mean that it is relatively ill-suited to the crystallized delinquent's needs. He would command respect and deference in the cliques following this pattern, but he would tend to regard their activities as innocent and, therefore, frivolous. If there were no criminal or fighting gangs in the area, he would associate with a clique conforming to the theft pattern, but through his influence, it might very well perfect its sophistication and skill in criminal techniques and eventually become a fully developed criminal gang. Thus, when conditions permit, this type of delinquent could be instrumental in establishing a criminal pattern of delinquency even where none yet existed.

In the lower lower-class such a delinquent would find little to structure his anti-social inclinations, and accordingly, he would not experience the same sense of identification with this class that he feels in the upper lower-class. Indeed, he would probably dissociate himself from other lower lower-class delinquents and their disorganized acting-out pattern. Not only would his puritanical self-control prevent his indulgence in their bacchanalian excesses, but it would also kindle a deep disgust for their weaknesses as individuals. Thus, if there were no appropriate upper lower-class gangs available, he would probably carry on his bitter protest against society as a lone wolf. But where upper lower-class criminal or conflict patterns were conveniently available, he would enter these and move quite readily into the upper lower-class.

We have examined here each personality type in the context of each delinquent situation and suggested the nature of the probable reaction. Although there is some evidence to support these suggestions, it is apparent that a great deal remains to be done. The meaningful articulation of each typical individual with each type of situation depends basically upon a qualitative comparison of the salient characteristics of each, and for this reason, it is not essentially an empirical question. Nevertheless, these expectations must be empirically examined to identify whether they are, indeed, valid; and furthermore, considerable empirical exploration is necessary to suggest those combinations of individuals and situations that have been thus far overlooked. Therefore, since the synthetic typology presented here is a preliminary version that will undergo considerable revision as more evidence accumulates, I have not undertaken to codify the several types in the same way that the ideal typologies of Chapters Four and Five were.

This synthetic typology, however, nicely illustrates

several important features about synthetic typologies. First, it is apparent that synthetic typologies describe the qualities of individuals much more completely than any of the ideal typologies from which they spring. They not only approximate actual individuals much more closely, but they also allow for a much greater variety among individuals. Thus, synthetic typologies have a greater ring of authenticity than ideal typologies. Second, although there is a distinct qualitative difference between each of the types composing an ideal typology, synthetic types often resemble each other in certain significant details. For example, the self-centered indulged delinquent adapts quite readily to several distinct situations, but to each of these situations he brings the same personal characteristics. Thus, a self-centered indulged child in the aggressive-exploitative delinquent pattern will show some correspondence to this same child in the theft pattern. There will be some behavioral similarities between the two synthetic types, but they will be sufficiently different to warrant their separation into two distinct types. Finally, this typology illustrates quite nicely the dangers inherent in a monistic explanation of social action. Obviously, the behavior of the crystallized delinquent in the criminal pattern cannot be explained fully in terms of a psychological analysis, although such analyses can clarify the peculiar intensity with which this type of individual pursues the criminal pattern. Similarly, the pyromaniac may or may not be welcomed into the gangs of the conflict pattern; but if he is, his peculiar behavior in this setting would not be fully understandable in terms of a sociological analysis alone. Thus, a synthetic typology assumes multiple causation, but at the same time it provides a rigorous framework within which several different levels of analysis can be inter-related without assuming the reduction of any of them into the rest.

A Synthetic Typology of Delinquent Groups

We have focused thus far upon the adjustment of delinquents with distinctive psychological orientations to relatively static situations, but to round out our analysis we must also consider the adjustments that each typical situation makes to the types of delinquents it tends to attract. Beginning with the upper upper-class mischievous-indulgent pattern, it would seem that since it does not appeal to nor admit any of the more seriously anti-social types, it would not receive much impetus from its members to develop in ways that are not directly implied by the cultural patterns of this class. To be sure, it might be tolerant toward the more mild forms of cleptomania, and through the influence of such individuals its activities in this area might be raised to a high level of refinement. But the absence of the more violent, anti-social types of delinquents means that in general its leadership is going to be routine and uninspired and that delinquency in the upper upper-class will not develop into a vigorous, adaptive movement.

In the lower upper- and upper middle-classes, however, we have an entirely different situation. The direct relevance of the aggressive-exploitative delinquent pattern to the needs and abilities of the self-centered indulged delinquent means that this pattern will excite and stimulate the considerable talents of this youngster. Hence, under his leadership the aggressive-exploitative pattern is likely to pursue many kinds of activities that are only vaguely suggested by its dominant cultural themes and to adapt quickly to the peculiar conditions and opportunities of its environment. Through the impetus of the self-centered indulged delinquent, it will probably become solidly established in the adolescent society of the lower upper- and upper middle-classes.

The criminal pattern of the upper lower-class would also be invigorated by the kinds of members it tends to attract. The crystallized delinquent would find his way into its gangs relatively frequently, while the self-centered indulged delinquent would appear less often and for shorter terms. Each delinquent, however, is capable of imparting to the criminal pattern a distinctive line of development. The self-centered indulged delinquent would be attracted to the more spectacular kinds of offenses, whereas the crystallized delinquent would be more interested in serious offenses that are threatening and embarrassing to the power structure of the community. Under the leadership of the self-centered indulged child, therefore, the gang would seek out notorious and richly profitable crimes; whereas under the crystallized delinquent it would serve as a medium for his private vendetta against conventional society.

It is conceivable, of course, that the two types of delinquents might engage in a struggle to establish their own particular style as the dominant pattern in the gang. Their interests are different, and there is no reason to expect that they would be tolerant or understanding toward each other. If it ever came to a showdown, however, the self-centered indulged delinquent would be most likely to assess the situation carefully and proceed in a realistic manner. The crystallized delinquent enters most struggles as if they were holy crusades, and consequently, he pursues his objectives in earnest as long as he is able. An accommodation between the two, therefore, would be likely only if the crystallized delinquent were able to impose his desires on the self-centered indulged delinquent.

Since the conflict pattern in the upper lower-class attracts a wide variety of psychological types, it probably constitutes a more formidable cultural pattern than it might otherwise be. In addition to the self-centered indulged and crystallized delinquents, it also attracts a significant number of unsocialized aggressive boys. Thus, the volatile imagination of the self-centered indulged child and the cold self-discipline of the crystallized delinquent is combined with the explosively violent manner of the unsocialized aggressive child. It would appear, however, that when all three types converge in the same gang, the unsocialized aggressive child would submit to the leadership of one of the other two. He would be very unlikely to prevail upon either of them to support his objectives, because his behavior is too irrational and eccentric to elicit the loyalty of types as self-sufficient and proud as these.

With such a variety of forceful, imaginative, and dedicated types to call upon, the conflict pattern could evolve in any one of several directions. Under the vindictive and highly moralistic crystallized delinquent, such a gang could systematically direct its violence against unwanted minority groups in the area, against schools and teachers, or against the police. But under the imaginative direction of the self-centered indulged delinquent, it could devise quite ingenious methods of undermining and destroying its antagonists; and with the vicious aggressiveness of the unsocialized aggressive child, it could become the scourge of the community. Thus, with these types to draw from, the conflict pattern could foster gangs that are a force to reckon with in the community. The seriousness of the delinquency problem, therefore, is compounded several times over when these types find their way into the conflict pattern and work their influence upon it.

The theft pattern in the upper lower-class is compatible with the interests and personalities of both the self-centered indulged child and the cleptomaniac, but here the interaction between the types would be somewhat less dynamic. The self-centered indulged child, for example, would enjoy the more aggressive and daring activities of the gang, although stealing as such would hold little appeal for him. The cleptomaniac, on the other hand, would find gratification in the group's offenses against property, but for him its other exploits would hold little significance. Moreover, he would probably have little desire to play a leadership role since the gang is merely a medium for the expression and fulfillment of his own private needs. The self-centered indulged delinquent, however, does aspire to a position of leadership, and he does enjoy the camaraderie of the gang apart from its anti-social activities. It would seem, therefore, that the theft pattern, by virtue of the nature of its members, exhibits considerable flexibility in exploiting the special circumstances that arise in its immediate environment. But we might also expect that there would be little endogenous pressure upon gangs within the theft pattern to change the nature of the pattern, except to adapt the pattern to the specific conditions of its situation.

Turning now to the disorganized acting-out pattern of the lower lower-class, it is apparent that virtually every delinquent type that occurs in the lower lower-class will gain admission to this pattern. Nevertheless, the anarchic nature of this pattern provides little basis for an imaginative expansion of personal predispositions. The impulsive delinquents all participate in this pattern, but none of them will have a lasting effect upon it since they continue for the most part to act as individuals in terms of their own peculiar inclinations. Indeed, the same is true of every type that occurs in this pattern. Consequently, it is not likely that new groups or new delinquent patterns would emerge through a dynamic interaction of individual and situation in the context of the lower lower-class. The variety of delinquent types found in this class do not coalesce in terms of social patterns; hence, there is little to stimulate them to become something more than they already are.

Some Concluding Remarks

Now that we are nearing the end of this lengthy examination of typologies, I would like to summarize what has been accomplished. I have tried to show how the controversies that have divided the Purists and the Empiricists in recent years might be resolved by appealing to theoretical insights advanced by, among others, Max Weber and Talcott Parsons, on the one hand, and Kurt Lewin, on the other. I have assumed with the Empiricists that delinquent behavior is a many-faceted phenomenon, although I have also maintained along with the Purists that delinquency can be explained comprehensively only if it is brought within the domain of a well developed body of theory.

The theory of social action provides a convenient framework for the study of delinquency for two reasons. It explicitly recognizes the contribution of psychological, physiological, cultural, and social forces to behavior, and it acknowledges a fundamental distinction between the phenomenon of action and the theoretical structures that are appropriate for its analysis and explanation. As it has turned out, field theory is essential to the explanation of action because it provides a systematic method of interrelating the force-systems at several different levels of analysis to explain the actions of both persons and groups. Thus, using both social action theory and field theory, it is possible to relate a complex phenomenon like juvenile delinquency to the bodies of theory that are most likely to provide insight into its essential nature.

In proceeding in this way, however, it soon became apparent that typologies offer the only manageable way of articulating different force-systems into a comprehensive explanation of empirical phenomena. The forces at a single level of analysis do not vary in a random or helter-skelter fashion; instead, they fall into systems or complexes of forces in which a change in a few forces implies changes in the rest. Thus, instead of single forces, the theorist must deal with complexes of forces, i.e., with ideal types. And since only a limited number of arrangements are theoretically permissible to the forces at a given level, the *entire* range of forces at this level of analysis can be accounted for simply by considering the *complexes* of forces that are theoretically possible at this level. Finally, by constructing a series of typologies, the implications of several theoretical levels for delinquency can be conveniently summarized and articulated to give a comprehensive explanation.

When delinquency is approached in this way, the mistakes of both the Purists and the Empiricists can be easily avoided. For example, it is possible to integrate social and psychological forces into the explanation of delinquency without falling into the error of reductionism or without confounding their significance to delinquency. Similarly, it is possible to relate delinquency directly to a body of theory without also limiting our attention to only one theoretical viewpoint.

When Albert Cohen pleaded so eloquently for an end to the confusions of the multiple-factor approach, he suggested that the relationships that have been reported between a wide variety of factors and delinquency ought to be brought under the purview of a general theory of delinquency.[11] This analysis has attempted to provide such a theory, but in reality our theory has emerged as a paradigm for the integration of several independent theories into a consistent explanatory scheme.

NOTES

[1] Karl Mannheim has suggested that the converging forces behind a specific event come together in ways that are regular but nonetheless unique to the event in question. They combine in lawful ways, but the particular combination of forces that produce a given event is extremely unlikely to be exactly reproduced at a later date. Mannheim calls these regular patterns of interaction, *principia media*. These principia media are fundamental to the definition of a synthetic typology of action. See *Man and Society in an Age of Reconstruction* (London: Routledge and Kegan Paul, 1940), pp. 177–87.

[2] James F. Short, "Street Corner Groups and Patterns of Delinquency," Unpublished Manuscript (Dated March 1, 1961), p. 22.

[3] Lewis Yablonsky, *The Violent Gang* (New York: Macmillan, 1962), p. 207.

4 In this case, he would resemble Gibbons' overly aggressive delinquent. See Don C. Gibbons, *Changing the Lawbreaker* (Englewood Cliffs: Prentice-Hall, 1965), pp. 92–94.

5 He seems to resemble in this context Gibbons' conflict-gang delinquent. See *ibid.,* pp. 81–83.

6 See Brahm Baittle and Solomon Kobrin, "On the Relationship of a Characterological Type of Delinquent to the Milieu," *Psychiatry,* Vol. 27, No. 1 (February, 1964), p. 13.

7 This type approximates Gibbons' "behavioral problem" delinquent. See *Lawbreaker,* pp. 96–97.

8 This type seems to resemble Clinard's habitual petty-criminal. See Marshall B. Clinard, *Sociology of Deviant Behavior* (New York: Holt, Rinehart & Winston, 1959), pp. 232–35. See also Gibbons' casual delinquent, nongang member, *Lawbreaker,* pp. 85–88.

9 This type strongly resembles Clinard's ordinary criminal, and in the course of time might well mature into his professional criminal. See *Deviant Behavior,* pp. 244–62.

10 In this context he bears some resemblance to Gibbons' predatory gang delinquent. See *Lawbreaker,* pp. 78–81.

11 Albert K. Cohen, "Multiple Factor Approaches," in Marvin E. Wolfgang, *et al.,* eds., *The Sociology of Crime and Delinquency* (New York: Wiley, 1962), pp. 77–80.

Selected Readings

I. The following works present the Purists' point of view:

SUTHERLAND, EDWIN H., and CRESSEY, DONALD R. *Principles of Criminology*. Sixth Edition. Philadelphia: Lippincott, 1960.
A carefully reasoned exposition of the view that social processes are fundamental to the development of crime and delinquency. Sutherland and Cressey are especially judicious in their criticisms of other points of view.

HARTUNG, FRANK E. *Crime, Law, and Society*. Detroit: Wayne State University Press, 1965.
A more vigorous and less cautious statement of the view that social factors through differential association influence crime and delinquency. Hartung especially takes to task the Freudian view of man and the influence of psychiatrists upon the law.

HARTUNG, FRANK E. "A Critique of the Sociological Approach to Crime and Correction." *Law and Contemporary Problems*, Vol. 23, No. 4 (Autumn, 1958), pp. 703–34.
A sweeping denunciation of several approaches to the study of crime including the sociological.

HAKEEM, MICHAEL. "A Critique of the Psychiatric Approach to Crime and Correction." *Law and Contemporary Problems*, Vol. 23, No. 4 (Autumn, 1958), pp. 672–702.
A painstaking analysis of the confusions and contradictions in the thinking of some psychologists and psychiatrists in the study of crime.

II. The Empiricists are well represented by the following works:

HEALY, WILLIAM. *The Individual Delinquent*. Boston: Little, Brown, 1914.
An early attempt to explain delinquency by resorting to the multiple factor approach.

BURT, CYRIL. *The Young Delinquent*. Fourth Edition. London: University of London Press, 1944.
A classic attempt to identify the relationships between a wide variety of factors and delinquency. It illustrates the eclecticism of the Empiricists' approach quite nicely.

CARR, LOWELL J. *Delinquency Control*. New York: Harper, 1941.
Carr seeks to develop a schematic formula for the explanation of crime and delinquency, using several different types of forces and pressures.

GLUECK, SHELDON and ELEANOR. *Unraveling Juvenile Delinquency*. New York: Commonwealth Fund, 1950.
A more recent and sophisticated attempt to identify the multiple causes of delinquency. The Gluecks self-consciously have adopted the eclectic approach.

TAPPAN, PAUL W. *Crime, Justice, and Correction*. New York: McGraw-Hill, 1960.
Perhaps the most careful and intelligent attempt thus far to utilize several distinct kinds of factors in explaining crime and delinquency.

III. The problem of levels of analysis is discussed in the following works:

VON BERTALANFFY, LUDWIG. *Problems of Life*. New York: Harper & Row (Torchbook Editions), 1960.
A biologist seeks to clarify the complex conceptual relationships between biology, chemistry, and physiology.

EDEL, ABRAHAM. "The Concepts of Levels in Social Theory," in *Symposium on Sociological Theory*. Llewellyn Gross, editor. New York: Harper & Row, 1959.
A philosopher examines the relationships between upper-level and lower-level systems.

IV. The best discussions of typologies can be found in the following:

WEBER, MAX. *The Methodology of the Social Sciences*. Edward A. Shils and Henry A. Finch, translators. Glencoe: Free Press, 1949.
The discussion of ideal types is developed at some length in

this classic by the most sophisticated sociologist to write on the subject.

HEMPEL, CARL G. "Symposium: Problems of Concept and Theory Formation in the Social Sciences," in *Science, Language, and Human Rights*. Philadelphia: University of Pennsylvania Press, 1952.
A foremost philosopher of science examines the role of concepts and theory in the behavioral sciences.

V. Several valuable analyses of delinquency from the sociological point of view include:

MILLER, WALTER B. "Lower Class Culture as a Generating Milieu of Gang Delinquency." *Journal of Social Issues,* Vol. 14, No. 1 (April, 1958), pp. 5–19.
The best theoretical discussion of class and delinquency available.

KOBRIN, SOLOMON. "The Conflict of Values in Delinquency Areas." *American Sociological Review*, Vol. 16, No. 5 (October, 1951), pp. 653–61.
The best discussion of the relationship between community structure and delinquency now extant in the sociological literature.

ROGERS, ARTHUR J., editor. *Reaching the Fighting Gang.* New York: New York City Youth Board, 1960.
An authentic and detailed discussion of fighting gangs drawn from an extensive experience with such gangs.

CLOWARD, RICHARD A., and OHLIN, LLOYD E. *Delinquency and Opportunity*. New York: Free Press, 1960.
An attempt to explain delinquency in terms of community structure and differential association theory.

SPERGEL, IRVING. *Racketville, Slumtown, Haulberg*. Chicago: University of Chicago Press, 1964.
An empirical study of Cloward and Ohlin's thesis as presented in the work immediately above. It provides the detailed evidence that is indispensible to the careful appraisal of theories of delinquency.

VI. Some significant attempts to understand delinquency from a psychological viewpoint include:

ALEXANDER, FRANZ, and STAUB, HUGO. *The Criminal, the Judge, and the Public.* New York: Free Press, 1956.
A classic attempt to explain criminality within the framework of psychoanalysis.

FRIEDLANDER, KATE. *The Psychoanalytic Approach to Juvenile Delinquency.* New York: International Universities Press, 1947.
One of the most convincing explanations of delinquency from the viewpoint of psychoanalytic theory now available.

REDL, FRITZ, and WINEMAN, DAVID. *The Aggressive Child.* New York: Free Press, 1957.
A detailed discussion of the psychological weaknesses of delinquents and a program of therapy for shoring-up these weaknesses.

WEINBERG, S. KIRSON. *Society and Personality Disorders.* Englewood Cliffs: Prentice-Hall, 1952.
An insightful discussion of the relationships between social patterns and a variety of abnormal behavior patterns including delinquency.

EISSLER, KURT R., editor. *Searchlights on Delinquency.* New York: International Universities Press, 1949.
An excellent collection of articles discussing a wide range of problems bearing upon delinquency from the psychoanalytic point of view.

FENICHEL, OTTO. *The Psychoanalytic Theory of Neurosis.* New York: Norton, 1945.
An authoritative and comprehensive interpretation of psychoanalytic theory.

VII. Several notable empirical studies of delinquency include:

HATHAWAY, STARKE R., and MONACHESI, ELIO D. *Analyzing and Predicting Juvenile Delinquency with the MMPI.* Minneapolis: University of Minnesota Press, 1953.
Hathaway and Monachesi provide a detailed analysis of the psychological characteristics of male and female delinquents in comparison with their nondelinquent peers.

SHORT, JAMES F., and STRODTBECK, FRED L. *Group Process and Gang Delinquency.* Chicago: University of Chicago Press, 1965.

A rather diverse but informative collection of articles focusing upon the empirical nature of gang delinquency.

HEWITT, LESTER E., and JENKINS, RICHARD L. *Fundamental Patterns of Maladjustment.* Springfield, Illinois: State Printer, 1947.

Still one of the best studies of delinquency. Hewitt and Jenkins identify three abnormal personality syndromes among adolescents and describe the family patterns that empirically accompany these syndromes.

Index

Studies
in Sociology